Everywoman's Guide To Time Management

Everywoman's Guide To Time Management

Donna Goldfein

LES FEMMES PUBLISHING
Millbrae, California

For my husband, Daniel, whose patience and understanding continually support my dreams and goals.

Illustrations by Gilbert Goldfein

Copyright©1977 by Donna Goldfein

Published by LES FEMMES
231 Adrian Road
Millbrae, California 94030

First printing, February 1977
Made in the United States of America

Library of Congress Cataloging in Publication Data

Goldfein, Donna, 1933–
   Everywoman's guide to time management.

   1. Home economics. 2. Time allocation. I. Title.
TX147.G62   640   76-54498
ISBN 0-89087-924-9

   4 5 6 7 – 82 81 80 79 78 77

CONTENTS

ACKNOWLEDGMENTS

My sincere appreciation to the following for their enthusiasm, sharing, and encouragement: Gretchen de Baubigny, Therese Post, Luci Orth, Nonie de Bettencourt, Martha Brigham, Ida Lyons, Marge Asher, Chris Bock, Sandy Bengtson, and the many Kiwis everywhere who have helped in gathering resource materials.

Special recognition and appreciation to Paul Steiner for his encouragement and legal assistance.

Also, I wish to acknowledge my precious children. Dana, David, and Dean were understanding of the many hours spent at the typewriter and their support was very much needed and appreciated.

INTRODUCTION

WHAT?   Time—

WHO?   For everywoman—

WHY?   Because most women give time to others—
children, husband, church, school, community, home, neighbors, friends, relatives and
sometimes even strangers.

RESULT: She feels frustrated, confused, used, and
exhausted.

ANSWER: A step-by-step program—day by day and week
by week toward the goal of—*TIME FOR
HERSELF*.

This book describes a simple plan that will work for anyone
interested in using time more effectively. All of us have
equal time and the secret is how we *control* and use that
time. Dozens of books on time management have been

written; however, few deal with a woman's special problems. Only a woman can fully understand the delicate balance necessary to satisfy all the requests for her time. She gives continually and often without recognition. However, each day brings new requests and the cycle continues. To direct one's life means planning, self-discipline and a perception of lifetime goals.

But who has *time* for planning and preparing a list of goals when the very thing people need most is—*Time?* You need the time before you can start the planning. It has been said that *life is what happens while you are making plans* and we all can witness the truth of that statement.

This book deals with the mystery of time. It will show you how time can become your friend rather than an enemy with whom you fight a continual losing battle. Think of time as a tool and with practice you are going to master the skill necessary to use the tool of time effectively. As with all skills, learning takes patience and perseverance. A first-time skiier is not ready for the Olympics and the piano student must practice for years before her first concert. Recall the first time you attempted to ride a bicycle? Not so easy—right? But, the moment you found the sense of balance you never forgot it, and your mastery of the bicycle allowed you to move the bike in the direction you wanted to go. This simple analogy shares the same message about our life direction. We are unable to control our life—control our time—until we master the skill necessary to use our time effectively.

In Paula Nelson's excellent book, *The Joy of Money,* she states, "A successful and effective life is the result of productive habits made second nature . . ." That is how I discovered the techniques described in the chapter which follows. I founded my program on productive habits that were part of my varied career as an airline stewardess, freelance model, teacher and sales manager. The balancing of these simultaneous careers had encouraged and even demanded that I use my time effectively. When I married, managed a home, became the mother of three children, and continued part-time work in public relations with an airline, these habits learned earlier were very much "second nature" to me. Women began to ask my help in organizing their lives and I developed my ESTE program, Easy Steps Toward Efficiency. I now conduct workshops in several cities.

The women who attend my classes are carefully guided in a step-by-step program in how they may develop this skill. Fortunately, it is not a complex skill and, as in riding a bicycle, you know when you have mastered the steps and once learned they are yours forever.

During the early stages of my business, I researched and read many books on time management, effective use of time, and other subjects related to this field. The "How-to" books may be theoretically correct, but daily living gets in the way of putting the often complicated advice into action. The skill must become self-generated in order to work.

This book will show you a plan that is simple and sure. Each step moves you closer to an individual system of planning and organization, establishing a routine that works for you. All of us have an equal amount of time—we all have just 168 hours a week. Why not start now to do what we want with those hours.

Budget Your Time like you were paying for it—because you are, in personal wear and tear and in precious hours you might spend doing something you enjoy more.

Women are often the victims of C. Northcote Parkinson's Law: "Work expands to fill the time available for its completion." Take the first step of this ESTE program—budgeting your time—seriously, and you will repeal the Parkinson Law. The next time you find yourself doing a routine, and perhaps disliked, task slowly—for instance cleaning the refrigerator, stove and floors—set a timer, rush to finish before it goes off and you will have budgeted your time which is the first step to *time control*.

Perhaps you are thinking, "Oh well, that sounds O.K., but it's a simple little thing and I want to learn about the big things that will win this battle with time!"

Let me ask you: Are you usually able to arrive on time each day you report to the office? Does an emergency call to the hospital ever get delayed or forgotten? Do you arrive at the airport in time for a long flight? The truth is that we do cope well with emergencies, with the big things in life. However, it's the many small irritations that cause frustration and emotional eruptions.

You may find it is difficult to rush something you dread doing. In some cases, it may seem impossible even to get started. Alan Lakein, renowned time-management consultant, gives this advice in his bestseller, *How to Get Control of Your Time and Your Life*, "It's particularly valuable stress the benefits as you plow through a long or complex job. You can give yourself a reward for working on a task as a way to coax yourself along." He suggests that the reward might be as simple as taking a break to read a book you've been looking forward to—or simply sleeping late the next morning.

Most women with the responsibility of home and family rarely have a morning free to sleep late. However, we can realize awards that are realistic and we must use them. In Chapter Six I suggest some meaningful awards. The first step of *budgeting time* is easier when we know the hours saved will be spent in pleasure. Adjusting our schedules to allow for such awards is not difficult once we learn the steps.

It is ironic that according to studies made by the U.S. Bureau of Home Economics in the 1920s homemakers then devoted about fifty-two hours a week to household tasks; a recent study by the University of Michigan's Survey Research Center tells us that women today spend fifty-five hours a week on housework—a longer work week than that of the average employed worker.

Dr. Joann Vanek, Queens College, New York, explains an interesting statistic to support our first step: "If women hold jobs outside their homes, they spend an average of only 26 hours a week on housework—less than half the time spent by full-time housewives. Clearly, the way women budget their time has something to do with this. Working-women have less time for housework so they do it in less time. They perform several chores at once, take advantage of convenience foods and products and set up priorities as to what has to be done and what can wait." Dr. Vanek offers a final thought in support of the woman who is not working. "The contributions of the full-time homemaker to her household aren't as obvious as the employed woman's paycheck. Although the work is important, it too often goes unnoticed—except when it's not done. Possibly, because the results of housework are so intangible, unemployed women work long hours to demonstrate unconsciously the importance of their work. Workingwomen don't feel the same pressure."

Today's woman is eager to find the time to do what she enjoys, to enrich her life. But the pressures she feels often cause frustration in seeking individual identity. The simple program outlined in this book will relieve the pressure and help provide the answer to her search.

Establishing control will remove the small irritations before they happen. You are carefully guided through the procedures of establishing an office in your home, reorganizing the kitchen so that it will be your friend and work for you both on a daily basis and when you entertain guests.

Do you have a closet full of clothes and "nothing to wear"? Join the crowd—but it doesn't have to be that way. The preplanning and preneed guidelines presented here may be the most important source of information in your life. If you lack incentive to get started or if you feel less than ambitious and need a boost, I urge you to turn quickly to Chapter Six. It will provide the stimulus you need. Final chapters will help you explore half steps to guide you toward those illusive lifetime goals.

I deal with simple basics and offer a clear definition of how you may create *time for yourself*. Once you understand time as a tool you will be able to organize your actions more effectively.

When I first developed my seminars, I planned them to be a step-by-step program so simple that women would question why they had not worked it out themselves. Ironically, the reason is, they haven't had time. To accomplish the goal it is necessary to take the time, now. The teaching is clear and concise and the message reaches everyone who is interested in using time more effectively.

For those not able to attend the ESTE seminars, this book will serve as a convenient self help course. The full program is unfolded from the first class session to the conclusion. To help gain the maximum result, take each chapter and set yourself a deadline for completing homework. Move along to the next item only after the completion of the first. Procrastination is an obvious timewaster for all of us and this book is not immune to falling prey.

There is truth in the adage "This is the first day of the rest of your life." Take the first step today and share the award you richly deserve—*time for yourself*.

One

EFFECTIVE USE OF TIME

One uses time effectively by doing important things now; not later. First things first is an excellent rule to practice. Lyndon Johnson, while he was in the White House, commented that the trouble with our country is that we constantly put second things first. He might as well have spoken for managers, housewives, students, professionals, salesman—in fact for everyone. We all put second things first by default.

Stop to think about the times you spend hours, perhaps even all day, getting organized so you can get to work on an important task. What happens? You find the time gone and nothing attended to but inconsequentials. This is a common trap and a difficult one to avoid. But, effective use of one's time is a luxury to enjoy and with practice, new habits become a way of life. The timewasters are gone. Here is how.

Ask yourself this simple question many times daily. "Why?" Whatever you start to do, stop a moment and think "Why?" Sound easy? Try it. The question forces you to become selective. Asking the question "Why?" will show you how often your list of priorities is really someone else's. You will develop an awareness of priorities that are your own.

A second word to help you use your time effectively is "no." The demands on your time will continue to multiply unless you weigh carefully those things you very much want to do and say "no," nicely, to the countless other requests. You will respect yourself more when you begin to feel in control of your time. The next step in understanding one's use of time is to be alert for the timewasters. Two heading the list are: Procrastination and Perfectionism. They can be evils in business, self, and in the home. Procrastination puts out a continual welcome mat for diversions. Perfectionism gets in the way of progress. Your life need not be a victim to these two timewasters. Everyone needs a system of planning and delegating to allow for less drudgery and more free time. Put a plan for the week on a large piece of paper. This scheduling tool will allow you to "see" the way the work is accomplished. An objective look at the paper will show ways you can improve and compress some of the work. This exercise is a time management technique and it is interesting that principles of time management are universal. They apply to any setting. To speak about planning, saying "no," recognizing timewasters, and focusing on priorities, sounds good on paper, but old habits do not die easily. It was nearly a century ago, William James, American psychologist, wrote a scientific treatise on what, until then, had generally been thought of as a moral problem: how to develop good habits and how to break bad ones. This was almost the first scientific application to problems of human behavior, and the essay is as sound today as when it was written.

In summary, there are three keys to breaking old habits and starting new ones.

1. Launch the new practice as strongly as possible. Tell your plans to many.
2. Go about the change positively. Whatever it is—changing the hour you get up—deciding to go on a diet . . .
3. Act upon the change. Put it into your life because a new habit becomes part of one's life not in talking but in doing.

One of the most difficult habits to acquire for home managers is to delegate responsibility. Unfortunately, the great "super mom" myth prevails as a result of failing to delegate. A busy household should function with a democratic arrangement of sharing and doing. Parents who do not delegate household chores are doing a disservice to themselves and to their children. An excellent tool that works as an early step in training and delegating to the family members their individual responsibilities will be covered thoroughly in the chapter on Establishing Control. Think of yourself as running a business and delegate with no strings attached. Also, do not delegate the janitorial work only. Remember rewarding tasks are important for everyone's self-worth so don't overlook family members.

Regular homework assignments are given at the end of each chapter. Completing each section results in "control" in a relaxed manner. You will learn to do things with a rhythm to life that will contribute to the security of your family and the pleasure of your friends.

Let us begin now with some examples of planning and the results. The external act of following a checklist and doing a task is the first step. The result is control and a positive attitude. For example: Setting the breakfast table the night before is an external action and will determine how you start your day. Your attitude is positive when you walk into a clean kitchen rather than one piled high with last night's dishes. Also, the external action of selecting your clothes for the next day removes the early morning decision of what to wear. Your mind clears for important thoughts.

Try a five-minute exercise program to clear the cobwebs; the goal of physical fitness will give you a positive attitude. Take at least ten minutes entirely for yourself and good grooming before you do anything else. This simple act produces a positive attitude and appearance for whatever the day brings, whatever the hour. And as any busy woman knows, there will be unexpected calls and interruptions each day. The "juggling" act is very real and very complicated but planning will help. Over scheduling your day is a one way ticket to frustration. If you will allow large blocks of time for important things, the urgent items will be completed automatically.

Now let's get acquainted with the To Do List and discover the power it holds. A well-planned daily list, containing urgent, important, short and long range goals, is the key to time control.

The busier you are; the more you preplan. Think about your habit of making lists! Expecting company? Holiday preparations? Planning a wedding, a move, or perhaps a fund raiser? Do you see the clues? When you are under heavy pressure to accomplish many things, the hand reaches for paper and pen. Here is what happens: Clutter and confusion is removed from your mind when it is delegated to paper. You focus on the high priority items, carefully working out a personal plan for the very best use of your travel and productive hours. O.K.? Now, the event is over and you go back to your daily routine—the list making is forgotten. This is human and only with determination to change and daily practice will list planning become a productive habit in your life.

Set aside ten minutes at the end of each day for planning. The result will be hours saved. Let me show you how. Keep the To Do List on a single sheet of paper each day.

Prepare a fresh list each evening and, transfer any pending items from the previous day to the new list. Toss out the old list each day. Advocates of keeping lists in a bound book miss the cleansing reward you feel by tossing away the day's completed tasks.

NOTE: Establish a place and time for regularly preparing this essential guideline. Use one kind and type of paper. Many students prefer three-by-five or five-by-seven inch index cards. Whatever you use be consistent and keep the list visible.

Budget your day loosely. Allow large chunks of time to avoid the frustration of overscheduling. Remember, this list is only a guide. It is not a rigid timetable. Any time we complicate our lives with detail, the effort is greater than the result and we discard the attempt.

To make your To Do List work keep it simple and brief. Also, reward yourself regularly for tasks completed. Place an Award Time on each daily list.

The To Do List is an imperative tool for mastering the skill of using time effectively. It removes mental clutter.

Take your paper and start with a simple format that you will repeat each day.

Phone Calls	Appointments	Projects
(Group together)	(State the hour)	(Blocks of time)

That's it! Direction for your life. Focus toward completion of as many high priority items as you can each day. Do not push yourself to accomplish more than you should. It is time that you are gaining and the time will be yours to control. Shakespeare has given us this message so beautifully:

> *This above all: to thine own self be true.*
> *And it must follow, as the night the day*
> *Thou canst not then be false to any man.*

and Montaigne:

> *The greatest thing in the world is to learn to belong to yourself. The same self-acceptance and self-responsibility ideal permeates today's psychology. It is not others nor iron barriers that we have to conquer or learn to control; it is ourselves.*

Control your own life and you will feel less need to control others. A lifetime can be spent in attempting to learn this lesson. Start at this time to consider "control yourself" as an ongoing homework assignment.

ASSIGNMENT:

Ask yourself the question "Why?"

Use the time-saving technique of saying: "NO."

Alert yourself to recognize Perfectionism and Procrastination. Guard against falling victim.

Break an old habit and introduce a new one this week.

Prepare a To Do List daily. Keep it visible and use it well.

Two

THE OFFICE

"Manage your home as a busy executive does the office." Everyone serious about time management must explore the importance of this rule.

The first step starts with "attitude" and your conscious acceptance of the truth that you are indeed an executive. Whatever your status: student, career woman, new bride, mother, housewife, single or divorced, an office in your home or apartment is a top priority and you deserve it. You are an executive and it is imperative that you assume a positive attitude. Accept and believe your executive title.

Have you a desk that is stacked high with mail, magazines you intend to read, torn clippings, invitations, appointment cards, reminders, and much more? The stacked desk syndrome afflicts more than ninety-five percent of all managers, according to R. Alec Mackenzie. In his book *The Time Trap*, he reports that for a number of years, when discussing this problem with other managers, he had approached it as well defined and self-descriptive (he too was guilty). All that was wanting was a solution.

One day he was interviewing a German executive and asked about the stacked desk, the executive, with a twinkle in his eye, said:

"It's because of all the things we don't want to forget. The things we want to remember we put on top of our desk, where we will see them. The problem is that it really works. Every time our gaze wanders and we look at them, we remember and our train of thought is broken. Then as the stacks grow higher, we are unable to remember what's beneath the top, so we begin to look for things in the stacks. So time is wasted both in retrieving lost items and in the interruptions occasioned by looking at all the items we didn't want to forget!"

Files

If you own a "stacked desk," or if you are attempting to operate from various "nooks and crannies" around the house, you must create an "efficiency center" in order to get control of your time. You must have a desk and files.

Combining things in category files rather than making a separate file for each item will save you time later when you look for something. Take the example of Joan who recently purchased a Caloric Gas Range. She stood with the usual handful of papers following the purchase and receipt of a new appliance: the instruction manual, the warranty, the guarantee, and the bill! Human instinct and natural impulse is to forget the paperwork. All that fine print, the completion and mailing of the warranty card and the keeping of all the details multiply with the purchase of each additional item and appliance.

Joan has decided it is time to "get organized" and she writes Caloric on a file folder, puts the papers into the folder and thinks a moment. Maybe this time they should be filed under "Range," or wait, it may be better under the store's name. Perhaps under a Service or Maintenance file would be easier. Joan has fallen victim to the "skinny file" and her answer and yours is to make friends with "fat files."

A "fat file" will be APPLIANCES and without a moment's hesitation, the full packet of information about the Caloric Gas Range, purchased at Macy's and serviced by A & H, will be dropped into the appliance file and feel at home with the packets for the T.V., the Kitchen Aid, stereo, and the new toaster. Our message is direct and our objective is control.

Another "fat file" should be maintained for each child in the family. The individual youngster's name goes on the file for the mass of papers that accumulate. This file must be cleared out regularly as events are over, sport seasons come to a close and so forth. When a child needs a school roster, Little League information, a class schedule or a full calendar of events for the year, the file folder with his name will provide the information and he can obtain it himself. No longer need you hear, "Mom I can't find the list . . ." or "Mom, what did *you* do with the schedule?"

To be useable a file system must be (1) *basic,* and (2) *simple.* If it is not kept simple, the old habits will win out and nothing is gained.

Creating the filing system is the first step necessary to clear the desk. So let's get started. Discard the thought of a heavy metal filing case and consider the advantages of portable, attractive, and inexpensive Sterling Letter Files. I am surrounded by three of them at this moment. They contain reference material, a collection of personal interviews obtained for inclusion in this book, and the third is a correspondence file. My three "walking file cases" give me control and save an enormous amount of time. Each meeting, class, seminar or workshop, requires papers and materials to take along. If it were necessary for me to pull these from a large, standard, filing case, the files would be in "control" of me and the time spent would add up to hours of wasted time.

Start a list of the office supplies you will need to create your "efficiency center" and top the list with plastic letter file cases. Any stationery store and some dime stores carry this "gem." It measures $4'' \times 10\frac{1}{4}'' \times 12''$ and rounded edges protect the desk and tabletops from scratches. The handle flips down into a recessed space when not in use. They stack beautifully and come in decorator colors. Aim toward a color scheme that is cheerful and comfortable to live with for many hours each week. A bright orange or a brilliant blue may offer an exciting splash of color; however, the choice of a soft blue or an apricot orange may provide the serenity that you thirst for after a hectic day.

Desk

By now, you are probably looking about and thinking, "Wherever am I going to put a desk and files and whatever else is suggested for this "work center"? Start looking and the space will appear. This is of high priority and will depend on the area that will be most comfortable, provide some privacy and will be recognized by everyone as your "think center." Hunting for the right spot will help stimulate your creativity. How about moving the large credenza that has long held court in front of the large, sunny bay window in the breakfast room. The second china set and company tablecloths can be stored in an old trunk that you pick up to use as an end table by your favorite chair. Or build a second shelf in the hall closet, above the usual hat shelf and presto . . . instant storage. The empty credenza provides new storage space in an upstairs bedroom and you may appreciate the change it gives to the room. As you now look objectively at the large, sunny window you can mentally create several excellent think centers.

23

Can you picture yourself sitting at a glass topped desk, supported with chrome legs, with lots of hanging green ferns from overhead. Like an oasis—glass and gleaming chrome with touches of living green.

If you are the more traditional type, you might take an old armoire and add shelves to create instant bookcases. For a desk, you may wish to complement the mood by using an old door in a horizontal position supported by wooden legs. This can be antiqued, polished or even covered to match the armoire bookcase. Line the inside with fabric or wallpaper of your choice. Here we have created storage for files, papers, books and magazines.

Another addition to this personal center that will be your key to effective time use is a typewriter. An excellent investment if you do not have one for home use. Place it on a typewriter stand with large rolling wheels. A small but mighty important purchase is a large wastebasket. The art of wastebasketry has been designated by management consultants as the most critical skill in managing one's work. An effective executive fights the tendency to overfile. It is costly both in time and space. The paper problem will be short-lived when how and what to file has been mastered. A simple rule that you may wish to adopt this very day is:

Handle a piece
of paper
ONE TIME ONLY

Think of the times you pick up your mail to open an envelope, glance at the message and put it back down to pick up another and, again, put that one down. Am I right? Next time you do this, stop and act upon the letter in your hand. You may wish to keep three file folders and label them "Today" (all correspondence that needs your attention immediately), one labeled "Bills" and the third "Pending" or "Future." Place on your To Do List the notation to "work on the future file" when you see a block of unstructured time and feel like catching up on that file. This is a fast and effective way of handling a piece of paper one time only. Most important is the use of the wastebasket. Consider it as the friend who cares. Place it close to your chair and aim for it often. The removal of eighty percent of what crosses your desk clears the way so your full attention can be directed to the twenty percent of productive correspondence.

You may find this statistic interesting and a bit awesome. "When people in charge of office operations were asked to estimate the percentage of paperwork in files that is never referred to again, the estimates ranged from eighty to ninety percent." This refers to large businesses and R. Alec MacKenzie reports in his bestselling book, *The Time Trap*, that some fifty million file drawers in American offices hold an estimated two hundred and fifty billion pieces of paper. The total mounts daily. Many household files are clogged with useless and outdated papers. If you have filing cabinets, cardboard boxes, drawers, or any other container filled with obsolete information and a system of filing that proves frustrating, confusing and made up of many "skinny files"—start from the beginning with us and see exciting changes.

If you have recently cleared a drawer, cleaned out a closet, or removed the clutter from your garage, you can remember clearly the feeling of satisfaction it gave you. We can do better when every tool we need to do our work is handy and put back in the same place after using. The key to this productive habit is not the size of your residence but how well you organize what is in it to get the most utilization from the least space.

Supplies

This list of supplies will grow and you will feel a need to keep improving on the basic design we have suggested. For instance, you may have many pencils around but, are they all soft lead and sharp. One feels helpless when three pencils in a row are broken or write so light you have to retrace. The same is true with ball point pens, marking pens, and pens in general. You can have a dozen and pick up three without successfully getting the phone number on paper. Over and over we are bothered by "little things" and these are the frustrations we can do something about.

The organization of your home is in the "think center." Pull that area together right away. Do not procrastinate or allow your desire for perfection in the desk or supplies you want to stand in the way of your progress. Many of the necessary items may need only be collected from other parts of the house. If file cases are too expensive initially, cardboard boxes covered with contact paper will suffice until you can afford exactly what you want.

Give yourself until the end of this week to get this area organized. Make a list of the supplies you will need. For example:

Desk light (hanging or clip-on saves desk space).

Stacking file baskets in bright colors. (6)

Sterling letter file carrying cases. (6)

Manila file folders (or consider color coded files).

Labels for the file folders.

Large labels for file boxes.

Scotch tape in desk dispenser.

Rubber bands of all sizes and a ball of string.

Desk scissors, letter opener, paper weight and memo pad.

Paper clips in magnetic holder.

Plain white stock typing paper and second sheets.

Three dozen soft leaded pencils.

A wall pencil sharpener. (This one item has erased hours of frustration for many . . . Do buy it!)

A kit of colored, marking pens which will have a multitude of uses.

An excellent pen to sign letters, business correspondence and your checks. Keep as a desk pen in a desk pen holder.

Postal cards.

A supply of gummed return labels or a rubber stamp with return address.

A roll of stamps.

Stationery to fit your lifestyle and envelopes with your return address are an enormous help. Create your unique look with a style of letterhead and envelope that is distinctly your own.

Business Cards

Another item which I strongly advocate is the business card. For those of you who already have the cards, you know the convenience and control they provide. I am eager to see more and more women place orders for business cards. Here is one of the reasons why:

Patty, a student came up to me following a seminar/ workshop and asked my help. Her talents as a teacher, musician, expert in needlepoint, student of yoga, and a multitude of other interests had fragmented her goals. She explained her frustration and as she talked I realized her lack of decision was the immediate problem. Katherine Nash, top-ranking career counselor, and author of *Get the Best of Yourself,* explains it clearly:

"Fragmentation is the curse of career building. It is an insidious ailment. It has destroyed more psyches, I would venture to say, than alcoholism—and, like the latter, it is probably a symptom of despair rather than despair itself."

Ms. Nash goes on to tell exactly what fragmentation is, and her statements concerning not knowing, vocationally, who you are describe exactly the reason my student was feeling so desperate.

I gave Patty my copy of the Katherine Nash book and said,

"Patty, think about the things you like to do best—the day-to-day living with a career that makes you feel relaxed, comfortable, and happy. Title that decision and have business cards made. Also, order some handsome stationery and printed envelopes. Do it and let's see what happens."

A couple of months later, Patty walked up to me after class. She handed me back my book and I could see changes. She looked confident, poised and happy. "Here is my business card," she said.

PATTY SIMPSON
QUILT MAKER
PH: 387-4555

Patty explained she had been happiest and most relaxed while she spent hours on her "hobby" of quilt making. Because her mother had been a teacher and her father a music instructor, she felt pressured to live up to their expectations. Although she had a degree in teaching she did not enjoy it and she compensated by trying to teach piano. All her confusion disappeared when she put on paper what she would really like to do—she took the next step of telling others and handed them her business card to support her avocation. Her enthusiasm was infectious and inspiring. When asked how many orders she expected to handle, she explained her first month was more than she could handle and she brought two friends in to help create, design and enjoy the new business. Patty is on her way and this shared testimonial is to encourage each of you to think about a title. Choose a business card and some stationery and see what happens. It will be exciting.

Getting Started

O.K. Let's stop and see where we are at this moment. You have a list of supplies to purchase or gather for your "think center." You have decided which area you will designate as your private spot. Our goal for the end of this week was to pull it all together and enjoy the results.

Let us assume we have gathered the equipment, the files and the file folders. It is time to place the materials into the files. Take the collection of papers, reports, children rosters, correspondence, tax receipts, insurance forms, and all the rest of your combined stack of papers and start to objectively think about what you must keep. Let me remind you to think of the "fat file as your friend," and the "round file" as your best friend. Discard all obsolete and the unnecessary correspondence and copies. Keep only the current and the essential papers. File in large categories and label each file folder. Place the folders in the letter file boxes and label the outside of each box with a list of the folder categories. You may have a tendency to relax a bit on this last step regarding the full list of folder categories placed on the outside of the letter file carrying case. You will negate the swiftness with which you can immediately find the paper you need if you fail to fully identify contents of each file box. Remember, with the "fat files" you will have fewer categories.

O.K. Now that you have worked your way through all the papers and placed the labeled boxes on the shelves, arrange your desk with your supplies. When your mail is delivered, recall the clue we mentioned earlier: "Handle each piece of paper one time only." Your first reaction to a piece of correspondence will provide a spontaneous and sincere reply.

Think about this a moment: "A postcard sent today is far better than a letter well intended." The thank-you written when you return from a party you thoroughly enjoyed will reflect your emotional high. Your message will be genuinely appreciated by the hostess. After doing this a few times the act becomes a habit. You will gain a reputation for being prompt and thoughtful.

The amount of mail you receive will vary according to your occupation. For the business woman, more formal replies are necessary. However, the tendency to shuffle papers, to type a formal reply when a note on the margin of the letter received might suffice, to overfile, and other timewasters may be robbing you of free time. Take an objective look at your workday and start to "budget your time like you were paying for it." When time is equated with money, the ability to look at this special tool becomes exciting. Whatever your avocation or status, you will benefit enormously when a forced self-discipline causes you to budget your time and save blocks of it each day for things you enjoy. You will be working harder so you can play longer.

Of equal importance to written correspondence is the telephone which saves considerable time. Paradoxically it may be an effective timesaver and may also be a timewaster. To control the waste you must learn how to terminate conversations. Rid yourself of the usual fear of offending the caller when you seem brief or busy. You are busy. Admit this and become a master of your telephone rather than a slave. Use postal cards in lieu of phoning when a reply is not urgent. Enclose postal cards with correspondence which requires a reply. Relegate these things to paper and you will feel control when you receive a group of postal replies vs. a similar number of phone conversations that will triple the amount of time to obtain the same answers.

Unless you are operating a business from your home, most calls received at home reflect an informality in mood and content. For the woman who wants to change this and doesn't know how, try this: Think about the two people out of every ten who call you the most. They may be close friends, neighbors and often they are relatives. Suggest a luncheon once every other week or even once a month to share your news. Also, encourage friends, committee chairman, church and school organization representatives, to phone only at a certain hour each day. Educating others to respect your request is easier than you may think. Also, the callback system as used in business offices will provide control by allowing you to make the calls at a time convenient to your day's schedule. For example, you are about to walk out the front door and the phone rings. You first hesitate to answer; however, the mental image of an emergency flashes across your mind and you reach for the phone. Tell the caller that you have an apointment and will return the call at 4:00 p.m. Schedule all callback messages within the same half hour and the discipline to keep the conversation brief will be easy. Women are often intimidated by the need to be courteous and gracious. Think about the inner turmoil and the price you pay for the continual hours spent on the phone. At this same time, however, it is important to acknowledge the pleasure of phone conversations you enjoy. Each of you have your personal reaction to the phone. If you feel it is robbing you of private time, stealing your morning hours, place a note on your phone with the one word "*TIME.*" When you are picking up that "ringing intruder" ask yourself if this is the best use of your time.

The woman who seems to effortlessly manage her home, care intimately for her husband and children, give time to her church, school and community and has relaxed time for friends and neighbors, has found the secret of delegating duties. She wears the title of executive and proudly demonstrates her efficiency to manage versus doing. Let me share an example.

Clara was elected to the position of Rummage Sale Chairman of the yearly fund-raiser for St. Monica's Parish. Her promotion was the result of six years of outstanding service during which Clara had helped sort, stack, separate, and prepare the clothing. Because Clara did not possess organizational ability, she hid from decision making and continued to work hours at sorting and tagging the rummage. As the date drew near, the obvious need for a good manager became a first priority, and the president encouraged Clara to form committees to do the sorting which would free her to delegate and to manage. Although Clara attempted to respect the request, she continued to redo several of the items the other members had marked. The result was strong objection—some even refused to continue working. The president had to appoint another manager at the last minute and Clara admitted she felt relieved to be "rid of the problem."

Companies often promote their best salesman into their worst sales manager. An academic institution often promotes an excellent teacher to principal and soon finds they have lost a superior teacher. Many times a mechanic promoted to foreman can never stop "operating." He personally takes on any job that looks interesting to him and consequently, he sacrifices managerial time. Because the title of superior usually carries an increase of salary and respect, the employee readily accepts the reward. But, the act of managing vs. that of doing requires a special skill that many fail to possess and often refuse to learn.

Louis A. Allen wrote in his book, *The Management Profession*, that a manager, when called upon to perform both management work and the operating work during the same period, will tend to give first priority to the operating work. This choice is easily understood when one recognizes the manager probably worked for many years perfecting his skill in "doing" the very assignment that he must now delegate to someone else. The frustration of having to stand back and witness a slow, sloppy, and insensitive job results in the spoken statement of, "I can do it better myself." Apply this to the countless times you have attempted to delegate duties to youngsters, only to find that the urgency to have the task completed faster and better causes you to continue "doing" and not "delegating." A sure answer to the letting go that delegating demands, is the simple act of walking away. Once the task has been thoroughly outlined and explained, the full responsibility must be given to the employee, worker, or child. If they are aware you expect their best and they are not allowed the luxury of knowing they can count on you to come around and fill in the area they conveniently neglect, the result will be a fully completed task. A manager who is consistent in his clear, concise, and realistic expectations will gain the respect of his subordinates. A mother taking time to train her child with the same clear, concise and realistic direction witnesses the confidence her child displays. Correcting the untrained child fails to "teach" because it smacks of criticism and is rejected by the youngster. A conflict develops in continual correction and a child often becomes determined not to learn. Recall our earlier description of mastering the skill necessary to control the tool of time? The training to realize this goal demands the continual repetition of a routine until it becomes a system in our lives. The same training of our children, our employees, our students, and every person learning any new skill will take the same pattern. It is up to the manager, the teacher and the mother to delegate the task and to let go.

We will move from delegating to the subject of creating. A very important rule in using time effectively is: *Create a place for everything.* Clutter breeds confusion. Congestion of one's space prevents clear thinking. A place for everything is a simple and sensible answer. The best executives are thrower-outers. Nothing is allowed to accumulate that does not have a real function. Learn to discard things that no longer have a meaningful part in your life. When we rationalize by saying, "One day this may come in handy," we are cluttering our minds and fooling only ourselves. It has been said that "temporary" is the longest word in the English language and a temporary location for that ugly plastic icebucket you received as a hostess gift is truth of this statement. Although you may think of it as temporary on your bar, within a few months it becomes an accepted item and although you do not like it—it seems to stay on because it has claimed a spot. Don't allow things of little value and poor taste to become boarders in your home. They are not providing pleasure and surely can't be considered friends.

Rid yourself of the strangers and surround yourself with open space and freedom to grow. Grow with new experiences and new hobbies. You may enjoy painting, but the energies necessary to set up an easel, pull out your paints, brushes, canvas, and all other equipment is enough to dampen your enthusiasm and talent. How quickly the creative urge to sew is put aside if you must assemble the equipment and put everything away again when finished. I do not mean to suggest you need a special room to satisfy each hobby; but do create a place for things that currently mean a good deal to you. The space you will find to do this is within your home. Apply the same research we did to locate space for an office. Find things to discard and make room for the currently important things in your life.

ASSIGNMENT:

Create an office in your home.

Wear the title of "executive" and learn to like it—to live it.

Purchase the necessary supplies for your home-office.

Design business cards and have them printed.

Sort and discard correspondence. Then file only the important papers in "fat files."

Put a *"TIME"* sign on your phone.

Start delegating and stop doing.

Create a place for the important and valuable things in your life. Discard clutter.

Complete this assignment if you wish to receive maximum results from the step-by-step program that promises you the best use of your time. It is important to set a time limit, perhaps one week or ten days. The pressure of a time limit will make you stop procrastinating and get on with the task at hand. In a week you will be ready for the generous list of To Do items that follows in the next chapter. *Hold on, here we go!!*

Three

ESTABLISH CONTROL

Control is the key to time management. You take control of the frustrations that bother you and remove them. The first nuisance is:

Keys

An obvious necessity and too often in control. How? Think of the last time you looked inside your locked automobile and saw the key securely safe in the ignition.

Or the frustration of misplacing your house key, losing the office keys, or forgetting your locker key. The many people I interviewed shared the same feelings: A sense of frustration, helplessness and definite loss of control. However, after spending money for a locksmith, or a taxi home to get another set of keys, or calling the office for their spouse to send over a key, the old habit of carrying only one key still continued in most cases.

Place on your To Do List a single statement . . . *Keys*.

Find a locksmith and have four sets of keys made. Place them in strategic areas. My students have proven resourceful in hiding a second car key. One young man explained he had an auto with a hood one could raise from outside the car. He put the key in the windshield wiper fluid bottle! Many slip a key into a magnetic box that attaches under a car fender; but, some felt this method unsafe. Spare keys in a wallet is helpful for both car and home because you will usually have your money holder with you. Use your own ingenuity as to where you wish to hide it—the important thing is to do it now.

Greeting Cards

If you envy the person who regularly sends birthday and anniversary cards, a few hours of homework can turn that envy to personal pride. Make a list of people to whom you wish to remember with cards this year. Once the list is made, keep it for future year's reference. The initial investment of time spent purchasing your yearly supply of cards will save hours of precious time. The frustration of waiting in line to pay for a single card, or perhaps two cards and being pressured by an overscheduled day is a common sight wherever cards are sold. Take a moment to look about you when you shop for cards. The faces of the customers reflect the anxiety of having to wait and you will see the cards they selected are frequently "belated birthday greetings." The guilt one feels from sending a belated greeting is a thing of the past with the system of yearly card purchase.

Treat yourself to a quiet hour and listen to soft music while you address each card. Place your return address in the upper left hand corner and pencil the date of the birthday in the upper right hand corner. It will tell you when to drop the card into the mail and will be covered by the stamp. The cards are stacked by month. Each day as you open and discard, file, and finish your mail, glance at the top card and see if a card is due to be sent. I suggest you allow about three postal days to assure receipt on the very day of the special occasion. Do not seal the envelope. You may wish to include a message on the day you mail the card to personalize the remembrance.

Occasionally, students tell me they purchase cards for one month at a time. However, the effectiveness of productive time use is not realized if you repeat this task every month and sandwich it between bill paying and monthly planning. Cards, like keys, are tangible timesavers when they are taken care of in one large purchase and the control continues for future months and years.

The Message Center

The Message Center is a time-saving tool. Avoiding Verbal Orders is assured with our Message Center. A message placed on an oversized calendar by the kitchen telephone will bring harmony to a household. As the family gathers for breakfast, a few moments focused on the Message Center will eliminate hours of frustration later that day. Let your imagination share in this scene:

Father has a client in town and will be late for dinner on Tuesday evening. Wednesday he goes from the office to the Club and Thursday is the special bridge party with the Shaffers. A weekend trip to the country is tentative and will depend on Jamie's tennis tournament since the afternoon is on standby status for Jamie's schedule of games and for Mom who is the family chauffeur. Speaking of Mom, she is expected to remember the above appointments, plus the neighborhood improvement meeting on Tuesday morning, the dental appointment for Jim the same morning and hopefully, she can spend a few hours at the beauty shop before the Thursday evening party. This is only a partial list of the typical day and week in family households.

The career woman may have an equally busy life; however, the responsibilities are related to her profession and the ability to organize numbers, addresses and hours on a Message Center is a convenient savings of time—and often temper. I say temper because this emotion is universal with everyone, regardless of their status, and the single or recently divorced individual may find the stability and the structure of a Message Center will help them to cope easier. Tempers flare when a missed appointment results in a lost commission. Such was the case of a real estate broker who confessed, "You know, when I started this session six weeks ago, I thought the homework was too basic for me. Maybe for a busy household of youngsters; but, I have only myself. Well, the day I locked myself out of the car, had my office keys on the same ring and found I did not have the client's name or phone number at home, I knew I had lost control. Just as you said, '—the key takes control when you have only one.' "

This is the kind of experience we all suffer and the guilt continues to hammer us. Let's share the support of a solution to the problem.

Lyn Tornabene, former editor and current writer, reported in one of her articles, "Behavioral scientists have clearly demonstrated that humans need order in their lives to function at their best. The order of our days in many ways gives us our images of ourselves."

Read that statement once again—think about it. Such enormous truth. Everything we ask you to do in the homework assignment is related directly back to a sense of order. With order, a close relative of organization, you will feel control.

To say it simply: Order results in Control. Control of our day's activities is accomplished with a plan of action. Remove the clutter from your mind, delegate the daily duties to paper, and you will have created a Message Center. The frustrating moments of repeating, "But, you said . . ."

"Now, how was I to know where you would be . . ."
"You did not tell me the time . . ." "I can't read your mind
you know . . ." "If you would only listen."

I repeat, time and tempers are saved by a Message
Center. Here is all you need:

One large, yearly calendar. (Spaces to write on each
date.)
One cork board to serve as the Message Center.
Push tacks, pencil with string, pad of paper.

Place the bulletin board within reach of your kitchen
phone. Put the calendar on the bulletin board with push
tacks. You will want to easily remove each month occasionally, turn to the next month ahead of time. The pencil is
secured to a long string attached to the bulletin board. A
pad of paper is attached and you have achieved what most
households need, convenient pencil and paper near the
phone.

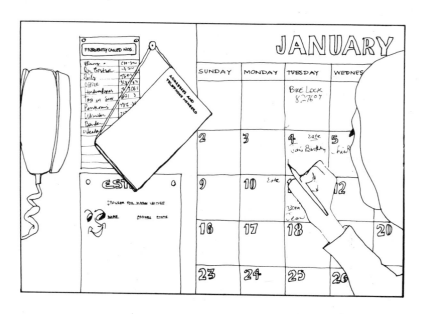

How many times are you speaking with someone and just as you start to give a phone number, a name or message, the other person says, "Just a minute, I'll get a pencil."

The person who finally locates a pencil and dashes back to the telephone may scribble the message on the margin of the morning newspaper or the top of an old grocery list which may be misplaced, and the lost paper has won control.

Start today with a promise to yourself. Bits and pieces of paper will be a thing of the past.

Address/Appointment Book

An Address/Appointment Book will work with you and for you. Let us explore the type we mean.

Place these requirements for your appointment book on your To Do List and it will save time when you consider the multitude of choices. A month at a glance provides a quick check of four weeks and you are not flipping pages from one week to the second and to the third.

An adequate number of pages for addresses should follow the calendar. Blank pages for notes will complete the book. It may be bound or a looseleaf booklet. You may wish to create your own in a looseleaf binder. However, they are readily available and reasonable. Purchase the booklet and begin entering your addresses and phone numbers immediately.

Always use pencil. The same rule applies in noting appointments on the calendar. A pencil gives you control— you may erase, change, and cancel.

Your personal Address/Appointment Book should fit comfortably inside a coat pocket, handbag or briefcase. That is a tall order considering the information we want to keep in this slim packet. It means choices must be made in the size and amount of material you carry based on what you actually need.

The size and the shape will vary according to your lifestyle. Don't put off buying one today. On your way to the grocery store stop by the local stationery store to pick up an Address/Appointment Book to suit your needs.

Without a single distraction, take the time to transfer messages, appointments, and meeting dates as well as addresses and phone numbers. Take the book with you everywhere. Once you have the book as a permanent friend and companion, the space it occupies will no longer seem awkward. As with a friend , it is always there when you need it. The To Do List goes on the inside front cover, secured with two paperclips. Slip any cards or envelopes you want to mail under the same paperclips and this full package provides control.

Secret Shelf

This often brings humor to our classes and students attempt to guess what it means before we explore the simplicity of "a secret shelf." Maybe you are thinking of what you carefully keep hidden and closed.

Our Secret Shelf is a miniature gift store within your home. Stocking up on general gift items for birthdays, anniversaries, hostess, and other occasions provides a year of thoughtfulness.

Occasionally, one might recycle a well-intended gift you receive and know you will never use. Make a notation from whom you received the gift and consider who would appreciate it. Caution . . . do not give back to the giver.

Last spring, a delightful mother of six children and member of a seminar I was conducting provided an unexpected program of humor when she shared her experiences of gift recycling. I had not noticed her until I introduced the check list item—Secret Shelf—and suddenly she stood up and shouted:

"Now, wait a minute—don't anybody start that shelf until you have heard it from one who has been there."

Her family had grown so large, so quickly, that she attempted to remember many things she admitted she should have written down. Often her children would receive gifts that were duplicates and she started to store them, untouched, high above the company towels in her upstairs linen closet. Occasionally a gift was recycled to the very child who had given the gift the year before which proved embarrassing. Her vivid descriptions were hilarious. She capsuled the experiences with this report:

"When I decided I needed more than white elephants and recycled gifts to keep up with my spreading brood, I bought a year's supply of toys, books, and games. I had the store do all the wrapping and the tagging of contents, moved the linen and put them in the same upstairs linen closet. Guess what happened? Within the month, I didn't have any gifts left . . . No, the children didn't take them . . . other mothers dropped by to purchase them and at a profit to me. They quickly learned it was faster to stop by my house than wait in a store. The business grew from a shoe string to my personal boutique which I still operate out of my home. I just wanted to take this time to alert anyone interested in starting a Secret Shelf that they just might end up with a great little business for themselves."

This type of personal testimony stimulates many class members to set goals for themselves. Remember the business cards? The first step toward achieving a goal is placing it on paper. If you are thinking seriously about something you would like to do, stop for a moment now and jot it down on paper. We provide guidelines for developing a lifetime goal sheet in a later chapter. Give some thought to this now and it will help you when we come to that homework assignment.

To clarify the Secret Shelf in a single sentence: Purchase in advance those gifts you will need for the year. It is a pleasure to shop in leisure time and to select interesting gifts for friends and children. By contrast, it is a chore to be pressured into the same gift selection when other priorities are crowding your day.

Emergency Phone List

The telephone is used for a multitude of purposes; however, the most important is that of calling when there is an emergency. Prepare an emergency phone list and place it on your Central Message Center. A duplicate list should be placed by a second phone. Our focus is to "keep it simple."

Take a five by seven index card and type or letter the names and numbers of: Police, Fire, Ambulance, Doctor, Dentist, Poison Control Center, Plumber, Glass Repair, Electric Company, Furnace, Neighbor, Pastor, Principal, Schools and Office.

Your individual list will include additional names. An excellent way to decide which numbers to include is to play an objective game of stranger. Think of yourself as a stranger in the home and all of the possible emergencies: a broken pipe in the middle of the night, a gas leak from the water heater, a ball smashing through the plate glass window. We shall prepare a booklet of information regarding the management of one's home and this follows as our next category.

I thought of calling the information a manual of emergency instruction. However, it is not just emergency information. More correctly it is a simple list of instructions; an instant guideline to give anyone caring for your home while you are away.

Household Instruction Book

This information will not fill a book; but, we will place the sheets inside protective plastic covers in a three ring binder. It sounds simpler to speak of an Instruction Book.

Let me share an experience related in the classroom.

An attractive, middle-aged librarian was eager to tell us about the crisis she faced the summer she agreed to house sit for her neighbor. The information necessary to care for the cat and dog, the automatic sprinkler system, and a few emergency numbers were given to her on hurriedly dashed slips of paper. The very first morning the sprinkler system started at four o'clock and woke her, the cat got in a severe fight and needed medical attention and the electricity in the house stopped when she attempted to open the automatic garage door. She was captured in a house with bleeding cat and the car locked inside the garage. The vet's phone number was not listed. She finally had to take a cab to an emergency pet hospital. A neighbor helped her find the fuse box after her trip to the hospital with the cat. She definitely felt a simple instruction book would have helped.

Put all the information for the daily care of your home on paper. MONDAY: What happens in your home on Monday. Does the milkman deliver dairy products? The garbage pickup today? Any service on this day should be listed together with instructions on what to do when you are away. For instance, if you are a family of eight and have a regular standing order of four quarts of milk, orange juice, eggs, cottage cheese, and butter, it is important the order be cancelled while you are gone. However, in case of an oversight the standing order might continue to be delivered. Get the picture? O.K.? Now review the entire week again as if you are a stranger caring for the home and need every bit of information to assure a smooth-running operation.

Putting this on paper one time will save you frustration at a time when your attention is directed toward planning a trip. In the event of an emergency trip, you may not have the luxury of even a few hours planning—it is often an immediate air reservation and off you go.

Think now, what peace of mind the Household Instruction Book offers. Prepare one for your home and place it on your desk. If you are delayed in returning home, a neighbor or friend can care for your home with a single phone call from you. List all emergency numbers and the daily step-by-step guide to caring for your home. Duplicate the same Emergency list that is on the Message Center. Additionally, give the service repair numbers for the appliances and all tradesmen numbers. This booklet is one you will regularly be using; however, it is all under one cover for the convenience of anyone who acts in your behalf when you are not home. The name of the game is *control* and that is your goal.

The last of our checklist items for this week's assignment will take you only a few moments. We introduce PACT.

PACT

Practical Auto Care Tips may save you untold frustration.

Is your glove compartment crammed full of old receipts, maps, messages and junk? Clear everything out of the compartment and place only the essentials back. Now take an envelope, or small plastic case, and prepare: Four index cards with this message: "Officer, this meter is broken." Slip four rubber bands around them and put into the envelope.

Instead of the usual frustration the next time you drive up to a broken meter, the preplanned message can be slipped in front of the broken meter and held tightly in place with a rubber band. Place these cards and some blanks in a plastic baggie, envelope or any small case. Add a small can opener, a bandaid or two, matches, postal cards, return address stickers, a pencil, paper clips, small scissors, your business cards and a roll of dimes. We call this gem Practical Auto Care Tips because everything it contains is so practical.

Many times you may find a few minutes while you are waiting in your car. Use it productively by writing post-cards when you don't have time for long letters. Remember, a card sent today is better than a letter well intended.

A word about the scissors: Pick up a small, blunt tipped, pair and keep them handy in the PACT . . . you will be surprised the many times you use them. Let me ask you the question I ask of every audience. "Can you think of a time you would rather have a dime than a hundred dollar bill?" The answer is, "When I must make an emergency phone call!" One feels helpless with all paper money and not a single coin to reach the operator and call for help. Only when we don't have one does it become vitally important. For the moment, slip a few dimes from your wallet into the PACT package and put it in your glove compartment now. Pick up a roll of dimes the next time you are at the bank.

ASSIGNMENT:

Keys—Take your set to a locksmith and have four sets made.

Greeting Cards—Prepare your full address list. Purchase, address, note the birthday or anniversary date in upper right hand of the card. Keep them visible.

Message Center—One cork bulletin board. A large calendar with spaces to write on, push tacks, pencil, and pad of paper.Write clear and concise directions to avoid confusion and clarify needs.

Address/Appointment Book—Purchase book and transfer all current addresses. Carry it with you and place all messages, numbers, dates, and appointments within the one book. Rid your life of small papers and lost numbers forever.

Secret Shelf—Preplan for birthday and special occasion gifts. Buy at leisure and place wrapped, tagged, gifts on your own secret shelf.

Emergency Phone List—Take a five by seven inch index card and place names and addresses and phone numbers on this card. Place on the Message Center by the phone in your kitchen.

Household Instruction Book—Purchase a three ring school binder. Pick up a packet of plastic protector pages for the typed or written pages you will prepare. Review this chapter for the step-by-step guideline of how the book is prepared. Place the book on your desk and you will feel comfortable knowing it is there if you must be away suddenly.

PACT—Practical Auto Care Tips. Put in small packet of the listed items inside the glove compartment of your car.

Congratulations! Why? Because your homework has been completed up to this chapter. Right? If not—let me outline the reasons this book will work for you when you do each step in sequence. If you skip the home office section, you will be distinctly handicapped when you attempt to complete the checklist at the end of Chapter Three. Every item is related to your desk and files. The order and structure of your home office provides a place for everything and alleviates all the clutter that spells confusion.

The promise of this book is to realize a goal: "Time for Yourself." Effective use of time is essential. If you are reading this book straight through from cover to cover and think you may get back to it later for the homework assignments—let me share the reality of what happens.

Your immediate interest to find the quick answer to time is a valid asset that you must put to use fast. Don't allow distractions to pull upon you and erase the results you will experience the day you start the homework. The time you spend speed reading through pages that will remain locked if you fail to do the checklist—is time you will never have again. When your first enthusiasm lessens, returning to this material will become a chore and soon the big "P" of procrastination is in control.

Don't be caught in the trap. Stop and take this gift of enthusiasm you feel about the concept of time being your friend and give it the necessary support to keep growing. Return to the summary following each chapter and complete all the homework. *Then you will graduate to the excitement of—*

but is seldom used. Most people have three times the amount of pans, skillets, lids and knives they can use. These freeloaders take up valuable space but people continue to move two pans they rarely use to reach their favorite.

Keep all purchases to a minimum and use the things you already possess to create order in your kitchen. However, the importance of sharp knives, a heavy skillet, and a heavy saucepan cannot be overlooked. Without this trio, you cannot enjoy cooking. To tear and pull at a chicken will double the time it takes you to skillfully prepare the dish.

Putting the unused items, including casseroles, surplus pans and muffin tins, old cookie sheets, bowls, dishes, glasses and old silver, into boxes and storing them in the basement or attic is an effective way of clearing space and gaining control of your kitchen. The drastic decision to discard or give away the items is avoided—for the moment. Surprisingly, the boxes usually remain untouched and nothing is missed.

Remember the statement: "Clutter causes Confusion." Keep this in mind at all times. Just as we cleared our desk to avoid the feeling of clutter, we shall clear out kitchens for the same reason. Remember: "Less is More." Think these two phrases over and over. In fact, why not do as we suggest in our seminars. I ask the audience to print them on pieces of poster board. When they start the Kitchen Magic homework assignment, they put the signs up as a reminder. It helps to focus toward their goal.

Take boxes, jars, and bottles of food products from each shelf. This is an excellent opportunity to line the area with a pretty contact paper. If you like the ease and the good looks of contact paper, but find it is hard to position—let me give you this helpful hint. Measure the area you wish to cover and draw the dimensions in pencil on the reverse side of contact paper. Cut the piece you will use; however, do not strip the full backing away. This is the point at which it becomes difficult to handle because it starts to stick to itself and to everything it touches. Here is the solution. Cut away only a half inch border of the protective back coating. The outer edges will assure the paper stays positioned and the protective coating remains on the reverse side to give double thickness to your work. Purchase of a full roll of contact paper will represent a savings. Measure the amount you will need for shelves and allow extra to decorate boxes. A small shoebox covered in contact paper serves as an excellent container for packaged sauces, seasoning mixes, and small items.

You will be pleased if you take the extra minutes to complete this task. Each time the cupboard door is opened, a fresh look will welcome you. Have you ever seen a large restaurant kitchen where each pan and skillet has an outline drawn on the wall so they are put back to the exact spot where they belong? I am not suggesting you draw lines on the walls of your kitchen but I do suggest that all possible wall space be used to hang favorite pans, skillets, and even lids. A well placed nail or decorative hanger may prove extremely efficient. The kitchen tongs, slotted spoon, pancake turner, long fork and kitchen shears should be rescued from inconvenient drawers and hung to the side of your stove. Presto! You will wonder why you hadn't done it before. One idea will spark another and as soon as you clear a shelf, clean a drawer, or hang a few of your favorite utensils, you will discover additional ways to help turn your kitchen into a friend.

Recipes

Are you in the habit of reading a recipe, tearing it out of the paper or magazine and thinking "I must try that soon." Do you try it? Does the recipe become a tried and true friend? Most family meals rotate approximately ten given menus at least eighty percent of the time. The other twenty percent consist of entertaining or eating out. No wonder meal preparation is a monotonous chore for many.

There are several ways to relieve the boredom of bland meals. One excellent help is to take a class in creative cooking. An instructor who is capable of imparting useful information and instilling enthusiasm for cooking provides great incentive. Class members are eager to learn and share their enthusiasm for preparing food. Cooking schools and individual class sessions are readily available and in all price ranges.

Perhaps you are a potential instructor yourself—put your creative talent to work for you and a small business could be started in your home or apartment. We are currently enjoying a trend of sharing services and exchanging talents. I encourage all of my students with a special interest and creative talent to consider a career. As you recall, the help of a business card developed a thriving business in quilt making for Patti. A weekly cooking class could be expanded eventually to a career.

The moment one crosses the bridge of disbelief in one's own ability and feels confident to cook with imagination and conviction—meals become exciting.

We promised several secrets to help in menu planning. A new recipe a day is a productive habit.

Care of recipes: Are you the victim of the standard three-by-five inch recipe card box? How many times can you fit the recipe to the size of that card? When the box is bursting with torn pages taken from magazines and clipped columns from the newspaper, it takes courage to face the confusion.

My suggestion for a working and worthwhile recipe box is a plastic box and white, unlined five-by-seven cards. You will need a set of index tabs and self-adhesive unprinted labels. These basic supplies allow you to take control of your recipe box and toss aside the ideas others have about your selected food categories. For example: Take the Biscuits, Breads, and Beverages or the Pickles and Preserve labels—you may never use a Pickle or Preserve file—ever. Yet it takes up the space when, for you, a Pie or Paté label would be more realistic.

Create your own file. Allow only the recipes that have proved their worth into the file; add to it regularly.

The new recipe a day will discipline you to select from the inventory of recipes you have in your old box. As they are tried, they are proven worthwhile or discarded. They enter the recipe box upon graduation. This may border on sounding dramatic; however, it helps to create drama in the simple routine of daily life and the visual image carries one along to completion. *Never in the Kitchen When Company*

Arrives. This is the title of an excellent cookbook by Theresa Morse, a small, fact-filled treasure of helpful hints and full menu suggestions. I am convinced the relaxed hostess sets the tone for the party. Staying out of the kitchen when company arrives is not achieved without planning, organization and timing.

The four basic principles of Kitchen Magic are planning, purchasing, preparing and presentation.

Planning

Your desk provides an uncluttered and structured environment to help plan a conservative, monthly, market list. Thinking and planning is time well spent and will save you hours.

Start with a list of the basic staples that must be replaced, recipes you want to try, and your best cookbooks. A continuous grocery list kept on the Message Center saves time and trips to the store. When the flour, sugar, salt, catsup, or pickles, need to be restocked—the note is made directly on the list.

Let us imagine you overextended your grocery budget last month and must cut back to help balance it. Forget the chronological listing of menus and tackle the list mathematically: number of breakfasts, lunches, dinners and parties you'll have during the week. The backbone of every kitchen is staples. Take the list from the Message Center and a quick check of the basics before you start. Think of four main courses, all entirely different, that you will create from one main meat purchase. For example, ham used in luncheon sandwiches following the last evening's dinner and small pieces used the next morning with a cheese omelet. Possibly enough remains to flavor a dip for chips.

Purchasing

Start for the market early to avoid the crowds. Guided with your list and a sharp eye for bargains, you'll be pleased with the savings of time and money. I wish space allowed me to share the numerous savings that are continually reported by class students. You will see the savings when you start a plan such as described. Don't waste another day to begin. Allow yourself plenty of room to change any given entrée to take advantage of weekly bargains. Treat the market list as a basic skeleton to be dressed fully as you complete the weekly shopping. Notice the word "weekly" has appeared twice. The minutes saved from waiting in long lines during busy hours will provide you with hours of additional time.

If space and budget allow, it may be helpful to purchase paper products, favorite canned vegetables, coffee, soups, and fruits in case lots. Consider the storage area under the basement stairs. Much of the bulk and the weight of our shopping bags can be eliminated if these items are purchased and delivered to the home or apartment. Often a yearly purchase is all that is necessary. The pennies saved quickly add up to dollars. The small luxury of having dairy products delivered is worth the time you save standing in line for that carton of milk or quart of orange juice. Buying dairy products for a full week can fill the space you must use for other perishables when you plan once-a-week shopping. That is why a delivery service is so essential and convenient. During the hour you will put your groceries away, add a touch of music but subtract any phone calls. In the regular list of timesavers that are collected during every seminar, we almost always receive this one: "Have an extension cord put on the kitchen phone." If you do not have one already, call today and have it installed so it is possible to move about freely if you must be on the phone.

Preparing

Allow a block of time on your To Do List on the day you plan your weekly shopping for an hour or two in the kitchen immediately following the marketing. Plan to return and set the kitchen timer. Once again you will repeal the Parkinson Law and you will continue to control the amount of time you wish to give to any task.

The following steps will take practice the first few times; however, soon a delightful rhythm will develop.

Remove the outer wrapper from the large package of ground round you bought at a marked savings. For a family of four, you may have purchased fifteen pounds of meat. However, too often the mistake made is asking the butcher to "wrap for the freezer please." The five pound package of ground round is a friend in the raw, manipulative state but becomes an enemy as a frozen solid block of meat.

As you attempt to quick thaw, hacking and scraping away at the block, ask yourself who is in control? It is important to take a first step toward the initial preparation everything you place into the freezer.

Discard the outer wrapper and take the favorite, heavy skillet which has been brought out within easy reach. Add a touch of oil to the pan, let it get hot and put five pounds of the ground round in to sauté. Prepare your favorite pasta sauce which can be used with casserole dishes and as instant spaghetti sauce. The best news is how we store it.

Fill empty, clean milk cartons with the sauce, label and freeze. Think about it! You simply remove a quart cardboard container, peel away and discard the box from the frozen block of sauce. Place it in a heavy saucepan over low heat and you are well on your way to spaghetti dinner and not a dish, jar, or container to wash. The joy of milk cartons is their availability in all sizes, in a shape that stores easily.

While the ground round is sautéing, wash your salad greens and place in crisper on paper toweling. Put away the remainder of the groceries. Depending on the size of your refrigerator you may wish to store some fruit in the pantry.

If you have a bit of extra time at this point, use it to save time later. For example, pour a pound of clarified butter into a couple of ice cube trays and you will have butter which can be used with high heat but which will not burn. To clarify, place a pound of butter in a heavy saucepan over low heat. Carefully pour the clear butter into the cube trays. The white sediment remaining in the bottom of the pan may be used to flavor cooked vegetables. Veal, mushrooms, and chicken, all taste better when sautéed with clarified butter.

Take another five pounds of the fifteen pound purchase and make hamburger patties. Place between slips of waxed paper, or flash freeze on a cookie sheet and slip the meat patties into a milk carton. Seal the top with freezer tape and mark clearly the contents. Now take the remainder of the ground round and add the ingredients for your favorite meat loaf recipe. Or, take a new recipe for a ground round dish and prepare a casserole for the freezer. That will complete the ground round purchase and you have spaghetti and pasta sauce, hamburgers ready for the grill, meat loaves, or a new casserole. Early preparation of each meal only takes a few minutes of your time and will save valuable minutes or even hours when you are rushed to meet a deadline, need a quick dinner for the children, or have extra guests pop in.

When your freezer is working for you, it starts to work for the entire family. Quickly they recognize the ease of slipping a casserole directly from the freezer into the oven or taking a few hamburger patties from the milk carton and placing them under the broiler.

Remember the poultry we included in our list of budget meals? Party menus include breast of chicken served a hundred and one ways. The first step is to bone the chicken breasts and this skill can be achieved with practice and a very good, sharp, boning knife. Ask the butcher, a friend, or ideally, the cooking class instructor to give you a lesson. Once you perfect the boning of a chicken breast in less than a minute, you will marvel at the savings of buying the entire chicken and realize a sense of control as you cut up and bone the chicken in preparation for a variety of meals.

Start with *Stock*. The wing tips, neck, rib cage and the backbone can be dropped into the stock pot, along with bay leaf, onion, carrots and tops and leaves of celery. A crock pot, so popular today, can serve as a continual stock pot just as grandmother kept a few generations ago. To store stock, cool it and use the empty milk cartons in the size you need. If you are single you may wish to pour stock into ice-cube trays. Remove the cubes to a plastic bag and use just a single cube or two when needed.

Chicken wings are delightful appetizers prepared as Chinese drumsticks. Simply cut the chicken wing into two parts, toss with a taco seasoning mix and place in the freezer in an ovenproof dish. They will be ready to bake and serve.

Always be in control of everything you place in the freezer. With this thought in mind, you will not fall victim to the frozen block of meat, the entire chicken with wings, legs and thighs all tightly sealed to the body and not providing you the convenience of using a variety of chicken dishes. Also, the drumsticks are immediate hits with children and the solid bone offers no danger to the very young child. The drumstick does have the very fine and sharp bone that rests alongside the larger leg bone which should be removed. Having chicken parts sorted in advance will assure youngsters of safe and tasty favorite parts.

Let's project our menu and plan for a company dinner prepared with chicken breasts that you bone and stuff with cheese, ham, herbs, or sweet butter. Bone the breast and place between pieces of foil. Using a rubber mallet (available in hardware stores), pound each fillet a few times and it is ready for slices of cheese, ham or your favorite stuffing. Roll each and place in ovenproof containers. Store and label in the amounts you will need.

This will provide an instant company menu when complemented with a soup appetizer (from the stock pot) and a crisp green salad (washed and in the crisper). During the twenty minutes it takes to sauté the chicken breasts in a cube of clarified butter you can cook long grain rice. Pop the chicken into the oven to bake for a few minutes while you relax with your guests. The effortless quality is achieved by preplanning. I have given only one example of a delicious party menu. Countless cookbooks focus on the theme of preplanning, and offer help and guidance to the busy woman of today. You may have a wealth of knowledge locked within the pages of the cookbooks on your kitchen shelf. If not, give yourself an hour to consider selections from the hundreds of cookbooks available in the bookstores. Too often a book is purchased and never enjoyed. Let the book share its many secrets and remember the first step is—*Attitude*. Create an air of drama. This brings us to the last of the four "P's" of our Kitchen Magic.

Presentation

Allow your creative self to come forth when you plan a large party or a small and informal gathering. Perhaps the most important time to be creative is in the daily presentation of food. The pure and clean lines of a soft boiled egg for breakfast is inviting when served in a sunny yellow egg cup If the toast and rolls are served in a small straw basket lined with a bright gingham napkin, matching napkins and placemats which were put on the kitchen table the night before—your day will begin right.

Setting the table the night before, setting the table early in the day before a dinner party, setting the table the moment you return home on a busy day, will create an illusion of the meal following soon. Very often this simple act creates a harmonious atmosphere and sets the mood which lightens and brightens everyone's attitude.

Above, I mention "create an illusion—" Let us explore the beauty of illusion when applied to managing one's life. Directly related to adding drama to the kitchen, it is helpful to master the skill of illusion in all things. You do see the comparison between drama and illusion?

A morning of food preparation can be turned into an illusion of your conducting a fine cooking class for television viewers. With imagination and a touch of drama, you will almost see the television zooming in on the plan-ahead meals you are creating.

Do you suppose the reason millions of people listen to soap operas each week is because of the illusion they experience? The program fulfills a need. An illusion is "a figment of the imagination." We can use the excitement of "illusion" to create something that is pleasant.

I think of illusion as an essential ingredient for Kitchen Magic. The extra touch of pretty placemats on a kitchen table, the family dinner served with candlelight and laughter, create a special magic. Master the art of illusion and you reflect a caring for those around you. You erase the realness of a day that was difficult and replace it with time to reflect about the good things in life. For many, mealtime represents the good time, moments of pleasure to share with family and friends. If you look to mealtime for relaxation and pleasure, discipline yourself to a program of pre-planning and projecting early. The results will be well worth the effort, and the illusion you create, a joy to all.

ASSIGNMENT:

Clear, Clean and Condense—Place a block of uninterrupted time on your To Do List, not to exceed two hours, on three mornings of this week's schedule. Check your attitude—set the timer.

Recipe File—This homework may take a generous amount of time. Discipline yourself to block the hours needed. Place a "new recipe a day" on your To Do List.

Planning—Allow sufficient time to do your homework—everything will depend on how well you have planned your menus, marketing list, and hour to shop.

Purchasing—Be alert to the best prices and allow flexible changes in your list. Remember a few basics will allow numerous variations of recipes that are "solo" acts.

Preparing—Block a couple of hours upon return from marketing to spend doing what is necessary to ease preparation at mealtime.

Presentation—This extra touch is like the finale of a great play. Don't deny yourself and your guests the excitement and the pleasure of food presented attractively.

Five

TAKE CONTROL OF YOUR CLOSET

"All these clothes but nothing to wear?"

People have been telling me this for years. The problem is universal and ageless. It is not exclusive to age, sex, or season. An answer is wished for by some and demanded by others. Come along! We will give you an easy answer and a continuous solution. Simply *Take Control of Your Closet*.

Too often, the clothing controls the person. For instance: You are late for the office and throw open the closet door, grab the grey flannel wraparound shirt and matching slacks. Suddenly, the mirror reflects the large grease spot from the salad dressing accident last week. Quickly removing the garment, you reach for the black turtleneck sweater but decide it is too warm for the office.

You have spent seven minutes and have yet to "find" something to wear. If the above scene repeats itself several days each week you are not controlling your clothes—your clothes are controlling you. The frustration and delay of such an early morning experience is a poor way to start the day.

Clothing should reflect the personality of the wearer. Comfortable and easy clothes are favorites and we continue to select the chosen few outfits. The clue is to focus on the reasons the favorites are worn about eighty percent of the time and all of the other garments about twenty.

Then why—why aren't the favorite garments given special attention and awarded a prime area in the closet? They don't deserve to be shoved between "strangers." Who is a stranger? All the mistaken purchases; the wrong colors, the wrong fit, the wrong style, or the wrong length. These are strangers and do not belong in your closet taking up space. That space belongs to your tried and true friends like the basic shirtwaist dress that takes you through many days and often into the dinner hour, and the comfortable pantsuit that really erases inches and makes you appear pounds lighter. *Remove the Mockery:* I use this phrase in class sessions and seminars because it *is* a mockery to continue looking at a crowded closet and feeling vaguely discontented and obviously distraught. Reaching in to take one garment and another and still another and not coming up with a finished look is frustrating. I suggest you continue reading the chapter and decide the changes you want for your closet before clearing of the garments.

Reorganize and Redecorate

You may want to take some reflective minutes to study your closet, space, structure of the shelves and hanging area. I mention this early because when we start the step-by-step guide to help you "control your closet" you will want the necessary supplies on hand to finish the task. Our goal is to make the most of the space available. As in the kitchen, we will remove the "freeloaders" and every inch of space will work for you.

Plumbers metal piping or a wooden dowel is an inexpensive answer to a second hanging rod for your closet. Consider a plywood shelf or two that may be covered in a printed chintz, a charming calico, or simply a plain fabric. Covering the closet walls, shelves, and even floor with wallpaper gives an immediate lift and pleasant greeting to you every day you open your closet door. If such a task sounds too ambitious, consider these possibilities.

Large airline posters placed like a collage on the wall surface and possibility on the door, or doors, as well.

Or display your youngster's work of art—the large butcher paper paintings.

A staple gun provides the most practical help if you decide to cover shelves in fabric. A full wall can be covered quickly and very inexpensively with yards of fabric or printed sheets.

A variety store will provide a wealth of stimulating innovations with which to work. Kitchen bins are ideal for hanging on the walls and the doors of your closet. They will provide a home for the items that don't fit on shelves but take up drawer space. When you bring out into the open many of the things that are hidden in drawers you will find them useable.

A couple of kitchen towel racks, also from the variety store, mounted on the walls or door of your closet will serve as permanent holders for favorite slacks, sweaters, scarves, and rope jewelry. A few yards of contact paper will transform ordinary boxes into organizers for accessories that may be cluttering drawers. Are shoes a continual storage problem? If you have tried the shoe bags, shoe racks, and shoe shelves and wish your shoes were enclosed but not inside shoeboxes—here is an answer. A five drawer, cardboard and fabric covered, chest of drawers. All the department stores carry these in the bathroom section or notions department. The initial expense is far less than a wooden set of drawers and the advantages are triple. You'll find them pretty, practical, and versatile. Place the chest in your closet. You will have a covered area for your shoes and matching hose can be stored within the drawers in plastic baggies. This eliminates moving from drawer to closet while getting dressed. The bonus of an attractive cardboard chest is the extra storage space it gives you for house guests. It is extremely lightweight and may be moved from closet to guest bath, to a downstairs den with ease.

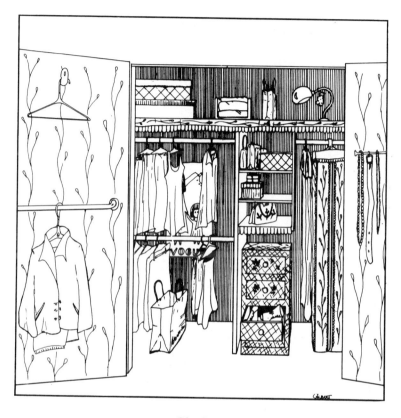

Clothes

You have read the suggestions for facelifting your closet—now let's take control.

Did you make the posterboard signs for the Kitchen Magic homework? "CLUTTER CAUSES CONFUSION" "LESS IS MORE."

They are excellent for this assignment. Place them near you.

Set the timer for a block of one hour of uninterrupted time. Take a break and if you are eager to continue set the timer again and complete the clearing and the condensing of the closet. The time this will take depends on the size of your wardrobe and the speed with which you move along. *Don't* procrastinate, prolong, or get trapped with the desire for perfection. Perfection becomes procrastination and we sacrifice progress. Many areas of managing one's home will fall victim to large blocks of "timewasters" if we stress perfection.

It often helps to ask ourselves, "Why?" The answer clears the way for faster progress. For example: "Why vacuum three times each week?" or "Why shop every day?" "Why" may be asked often. The answers may shock you. You are doing repeat patterns of managing a home that may have become obsolete, possibly, following the example of a parent, or a teacher. Admittedly, there is a time and place for perfection. I simply encourage you to carefully weigh the decision and in the case of our Wardrobe Homework Assignment the goal is to complete the task within the time you have allotted.

Remove each article of clothing. Ask yourself "Why?" Focus on why it is taking up space in your closet—why you are not wearing it often, or perhaps at all—why do you keep it?

Are you thinking that if you get rid of all the things you don't wear often, don't like, or that don't fit, you will have an empty closet? Be assured I will not suggest that you get rid of all your clothes. You might very well want them back next week, next month or even tomorrow.

However, I definitely suggest that you remove from your sight the eighty percent of your clothing that you only occasionally wear and for which you feel aggravation and a sense of guilt. The reasons for not wearing them will vary; however, there seem to be repetitive patterns. It is my aim to alert you to the reasons and you may save yourself mistakes in the future.

What mistakes? The error of "buying on impulse," "buying to fill time" and "buying under pressure."

A well coordinated, planned and projected wardrobe is the result of homework done well. The key to a working wardrobe is garments which match one another. It takes some planning. That does not just happen.

Rosemary Stack, wife of actor Robert Stack, reported her wardrobe is mostly classics because she believes clothes are an investment and should last for a long time.

One's personality determines the type of clothing she prefers, and most importantly, the type that looks well. Perhaps you enjoy a classic style, varied on occasion with something currently vogue. The first step is understanding what you wear best. This will help you to avoid wrong purchases.

Carefully, but quickly, go through every garment hanging in your closet and start to place the clothing in categories. You may have a problem in where to put them for this period of sorting. Ideally, a clothes rack would help, however, few homes have one so simply place a stack over a chair, on a sofa, and the largest group can rest temporarily on the bed.

This reminds me of when an enthusiastic student who dashed home following our wardrobe class and started to clear her closet. It was late afternoon and she was called to pick up her son from a Little League game. She came back and had to prepare the dinner for her family of five. Later that evening her husband walked into the bedroom, found her clothes all over the bed and thought she was packing to leave him. I caution you to select a time of day, preferably morning, and arrange not to be interrupted until the clothes can be picked up and replaced somewhere. Somewhere may be back in the closet, if you want, but, let us consider the different categories and the size of the stacks we now have.

You have asked the question "Why?" and sometimes you may have had a question. There seem to be many "maybe's" like, "Well, maybe one day I will wear this" or "Maybe if I lose five pounds."

In brief, the "maybe's" are not the "for sures" and only sure things belong. Realistically, it is a struggle to make an instant decision to store, to sell, to give away the "maybes."

Concentrate on the "for sure" category. Put these on the hanging rack of your closet and study them for "uniform sets." Mix and match, coordinating the basics with an eye alert for ways of wearing your favorites you may have over-looked. Often a blouse, sweater, or a pair of slacks you have overlooked for many months will appear as a fine complement to a favorite basic and you will have "found" a new outfit. Use your creativity to assemble as many coor-dinated looks as you can. Be sure the garments you select as your working wardrobe are all ready for wear. Check buttons, snaps, and fasteners as well as anything that needs to be laundered or go to the cleaners. In brief: Be certain the entire group is ready for wear.

The least amount returned to the closet—the better. However, for all the things you think you may be needing, wearing, and using—sometimes—put them toward the back of the closet and pin a large sheet about them.

Why? Because they have no right to continue confusing you and causing guilt for having purchased them and not wearing them. Better to recognize the mistake and remove it from your view. The sheet will do this and if you should need a garment, it is available. Slowly, those items under the sheet will find their way to the church bazaar, thrift shops, and the Good Will box.

Discard the mistakes: We spoke of the slow removal of the items resting under the sheet and how in time they will be discarded. However, the next time you purchase what you think will be perfect and is not—see if you can return the garment immediately. If not, recognize the error and clear it from your closet before it builds into the very clutter we have removed. When you are shopping remember the past mistakes and attempt to avoid them.

Any attractive basic that you now have in your wardrobe may have matching accessories that are perfect. Everything seems to belong and most likely you purchased it as a unit. You were wearing the pantsuit, or the three piece plaid daytime suit, when you paired it with the right sweater, blouse, belt and scarf.

When shopping wear any two items that represent the basic (hence the skirt and jacket, the pant and vest, the slacks and shirt). Because the range of colors and degrees of tone in addition to the importance of texture and weight of clothing, it is an expensive gamble to attempt to match a color by memory. Only if you are wearing the "basic," can you be certain the new purchase will look perfectly coordinated. When it seems inconvenient to wear the "basic" during a shopping trip, slip it into a shopping bag and again you will be in full control.

This is equally as important when shopping for shoes. If you already have the shoes and wish to coordinate the right look, it is not enough to know they are black, brown or navy. The height and shape of the heel and the very way they look with the length of skirt or the flare of the pant will result in a look that is either great or just missing.

If you have invested in good leather boots, I caution you to always wear them when shopping for a total look. The effect can be "smashing" when the costume look prevails; but a haphazard collection of separates will make a pair of boots look awkward and heavy.

Perhaps you already practice this successful way of planned shopping and realize the benefits. For any of you whose closets have been filled with mismatches and impulse purchases, you will save both time and money, and discipline is an added bonus as you become aware of the pitfalls of buying under pressure, impulse or boredom.

Packing for Travel

My professional affiliation in the travel field has provided me with twenty years' experience in packing for travel. The hundreds of potential travelers, who are my audience during packing seminars, continue to ask the same questions.

"How can I pack less—I want to travel lighter and end up taking twice the amount I actually need—what is the secret to packing for a four week trip?"

The answer is simple and using the same key phrases we did when cleaning the closet, you must be cautious about the "ifs" and the "maybes." Only the "for sures" are paying their way on your trip. Everything you pack must stand the test of being a friend, having a buddy, and earning its way into the case.

These three prerequisites will be explored as we share hints and suggestions on packing for travel.

"For sures" represent the "friends" and any garments we enjoy wearing, are comfortable, and serve us well, are "friends." The friend will pair well with other items and coordinate to make several ensembles. This is the "buddy system" and every piece packed should have a buddy. A lone garment that demands its own shoes, scarf, and handbag is not working as a buddy.

Let us pack now for the ten day trip. If your closet has just felt the changes of the completed homework assignment, the job is easy. Packing will be a cinch because most of the decisions have been made. Let us think positive—the homework has been completed and let's assume you live on the West Coast. You are about to pack for an East Coast Holiday.

A knit that travels well, matched with a cape or poncho, offers a layered look and is an excellent choice. You may need the warmth for the cooler weather and you can easily carry the cape or poncho arriving on the East Coast. Select your shoes for comfort and coordination with almost everything you pack. Ideally, a pair to wear and one to pack. If you are planning on tennis, jogging, or any athletic activity during your vacation—pack accordingly.

Take the items you think you will need and put them on your bed. Each time you take a hanger from the closet and you think these words . . . "Maybe I will"—or—"If I go"—return the hanger to the closet. All of the "maybes" and the "ifs" are a gamble and have not really earned their way into your suitcase.

Consider only the "for sures" and with these in front of you, take a pencil and paper and make a list. List basics on the left and accessories on the right. To give you a clearer picture of the help this list will give in packing I will share a recent wardrobe I took to London for a two week holiday. I also stopped in New York for a week before returning home to San Francisco. The entire wardrobe fit into a small, under-the-seat case that I carried on all the flights and avoided hours of waiting in line for luggage and clearing customs. My young son and I were the first in line going through customs and caught the first taxi into the city before others had collected their bags. Although it may not always be possible to pack in small cases, it is worth the effort if you possibly can.

BASICS	ACCESSORIES

1 Copper colored jacket, finger tip length in light weight wool. [2, 3, a]

2 Knit gored, rust colored skirt with elastic waistband. [1, a, e, f, h]

3 Polyester, rust colored pants and matching vest. [1, a, d, e, h]

4 Black/white, houndstooth slacks. [b, d, g]

5 Black, lightweight crepe evening slacks. [e, g]

6 Classic, one piece evening dress of nylon jersey. [b, g]

7 Indian cotton, wrap around skirt in multi-colored rust, yellow and orange. [c, d, h]

8 Bermuda walking shorts in classic Scotch plaid. [c, d, h]

9 Nightgown, robe and slippers.

a Rust, suede shoes, medium heel, closed pump.

b Black, medium heel sandal. (Perfect with evening gown, black slacks, b/white slacks, and the multi-colored wrap skirt).

c Walking shoes for lots of touring and the country. (Use with the bermuda shorts, slacks, and the multi-colored wrap skirt.)

d Cotton T-shirts in orange, yellow, white, eggshell and black.

e Easy-care long sleeved blouses in white and beige.

f One long sleeved, light wool sweater in black.

g Evening sweater cardigan in black and silver. May be used with blouse or as top with jewelry.

h Several scarves in colors to complement rust, black, white and yellow. Cotton squares to cover hair and a few pieces of jewelry.

ASSIGNMENT:

Reorganize and Redecorate—Place on your To Do List the supplies you will need to refurbish your closet. Support your own ideas with visual aids from magazines and decorating books.

Clothes—Block time this week, preferably morning, to clear and condense your closet.

Packing for Travel—Start with a small case. Prepare a master list after you have selected the "for sure" items. Cross reference basics with accessories on paper.

A popular bit of advice is to pack your suitcases—turn around and take out half and leave it at home. Double the amount of money instead and you will be certain of a top rate vacation.

It is easy to agree with the thought but, not always possible to double the money. Realistically, you will not want to carry around heavy suitcases that are filled with clothing that has not earned its way into the case. *Keep in mind "Less is More" and you will do fine.*

Six

TIME FOR YOURSELF

Time for Yourself—is that what you want? You deserve it and the focus of this material is to help you realize that goal. *Time for Yourself*—sounds good, doesn't it? The hours each day that you can claim as your very own; guilt free hours that are rightfully yours to spend as you choose.

Many times I hear women's reactions, uttered in a variety of ways but sharing the same discovery.

"For the first time in years, I am taking the time to know myself. I had smothered the 'real me' under layers of responsibilities to others."

"Every day I am finding out something new about myself—something that used to be me—and with the freedom of hours to discover *my* wants and *my* likes I keep finding a freshness about me that I like—it's fun."

"Until I felt honest about taking time for myself, I purposely filled every day with "busy work" and hid behind the wall of martyrdom. The first days of taking an hour for myself, still had me hiding. I hid the truth that I was doing something for me—just me. Only when my personality reflected the change could I accept the fact it was good for me to plan each day with the priority of having "time for myself."

What self-inflicted dedication to others has erased the importance of doing for yourself?

The underlying theme seems to be the inability to say no nicely. Many women have developed the habit of saying yes to the countless demands upon their time. It takes courage to change habits you have lived with for many years. Friends, business associates, husband, and children all expect top priority. Because of this a woman often feels she must *justify* spending time on herself.

The volumes that have been written about the rapid changes in women's roles today are encouraging for the thousands who are making major changes. However, the enormous, silent majority may not wish to make major changes in their life—but rather adjustments within their lifestyle. Many feel trapped by repetitive routines and daily demands upon their time. These women find the answer in learning to know themselves.

Perhaps that statement sounds trite but the enormity of getting to know and understand yourself and your abilities can be complex and confusing. Today is not too soon to start. Are you aware of how often we accept a person because of her acceptance of herself? Some people possess the maturity to accept what they are without continually attempting to copy someone else or change. Others attempt to mirror the dress, hairstyle, and even the speech of another. We tend to accept this behavior in teenagers and understand they are seeking identity, however, the adult who follows a pattern of searching for an image that is a carbon copy of another is being unfair to herself and to all those around her.

However, to wake up one day and realize you really don't know who you are, what you truly want, and where you are going, is the awakening that seems to be racing across the nation. Books, newspapers, magazines, and television talk shows are devoting a lot of space and time to the subject of "Who am I?"

A simple and available program to everyone is an Award System. The award is an hour a day to spend in a way that gives pleasure and relaxation. The Award a day is the first homework assignment given to every student taking the class. The idea is exciting but it requires discipline to take the hour each day. You will not "find" the hour. It is only with the control of your time that you can routinely give to yourself the hour that is most important to your day and to your life.

Note on your To Do List "Award Time." Think of "Award Time" as time each day to take inventory of yourself and your physical and emotional needs.

Daydreams

Do you daydream? Do you equate daydreaming with "wasting time." Perhaps a teacher, years ago, cautioned you with a threat about the dire consequences of your tendency to "daydream," or, your parents repeatedly told you to "Stop daydreaming and get busy."

The idea that it is bad to spend time in this way is a throw-back to the "Puritan work ethic"—in truth, wasted time is simply unstructured time, free of demands.

To daydream is to relax, to drift, to enjoy the world of fantasy. The experience can tell you many things that you may never have known about yourself.

When you daydream, the protective shield is pushed aside. Like peeling an orange, you are peeling away layers of insulation and allowing an unfocused and unreal dream to play upon your imagination. Every human possesses an unconscious reservoir of creativity and often a daydream serves to release a desire, an idea, that flows into the world of reality. At that moment, you can seize upon the idea and direct it to serve you in a constructive and productive way that may change the direction of your life.

This process really works and I have collected numerous real life examples to support the importance of daydreaming. Here are a few I would like to share taken from a cross-section of groups:

Amy, a social worker, was involved in a pattern of continuous giving. Because her mother was widowed shortly following Amy's graduation from high school, it was expected that she continue to live at home for a while. The months passed into years.

"I never felt comfortable about daydreaming. Until your class I would catch myself daydreaming and feel guilty. It seemed like I always had to force myself to get busy doing something to take my mind off the delightful fantasies."

The happy conclusion of Amy's daydreams was the discovery of her hidden desire of wanting to be alone, to have an apartment she could decorate and the privacy to come and go without reporting her actions to anyone. She yearned for the total silence of a room without voices after a day filled with the endless questions related to her work.

The happy conclusion in this case was the discovery that her mother was delighted to change the arrangements. She had felt the need for more freedom also, but felt tied down to "making a home" for her daughter. They both glowed with mutual respect that each seemed to have for the other.

A teenager who attended a day seminar gave a revealing report. He had practiced the daily Award Time each day for a month. Every fourth day, he purposely spent the time daydreaming. He learned many things about himself that surprised and even scared him a little. He realized he had agreed to a course of study to please his counselor and one which he really didn't want to follow.

The answer was simple. Once recognized, he took control of the situation and told the teacher his feelings. Together they quickly put a new course of study into action.

Many personal reports about daydreaming were repetitive. The new found freedom of taking up art or writing again—classes in yoga, modeling, acting, flower arranging, cake decorating, and swimming for the first time. Collectively speaking, many creative talents were allowed to surface and the result was always positive.

I found something else that gives great support to the importance of daydreaming—hidden skills women had secretly hoped to master someday. In many, many cases the Award Time provided time for interests people had given up.

"All my life I have dreamed about speaking fluent French." or—

"I never learned to drive and my husband keeps saying it isn't necessary. Every year I feel less confident about learning—" This woman was driving within three months. She used the Award Time.

"How I wanted to play the piano—ever since I was a little girl and only my sister was given lessons." Again, the daydreaming brought the desire to the surface and the regular time for herself made the dream a reality.

The purpose of sharing these stories is to encourage you to explore the great world of fantasy. Take a few minutes this very moment—put the book down and daydream.

Plan a Ten Year Goal Sheet

Goal planning is a popular topic of conversation in classes, seminars, living rooms, and college dorms. There are many pros and cons, as well as suggested rules and methods to chart your goals.

I am convinced the average person will put aside any plan that is overly complicated; it's only human.

A mood of lightness is noticeable in the classroom situation when we begin to discuss the subject of establishing goals. You may wish to do this alone, with family or possibly friends whom you enjoy and whose judgment you respect. It is important to set a mood.

Close your eyes and imagine you are walking into a room filled with comfortable sofas and thick carpeting. The soft down cushions of the sofa welcome you to relax and forget the day. As you look around even the walls are covered with the same white velvet as the pillows and it produces a lovely feeling of cleanness and comfort.

Keep your eyes closed now and think about the future. If you could do anything you'd like, what would you do? Is the something you are thinking about possible for you to do? How long would it take to achieve the particular thing you would like to do? Think about the ways you might achieve the goal. If it is too remote or possibly unrealistic—shift to another goal.

If you are doing this with others, after some time has been devoted to thinking individually, and many goals have been considered, you may want to discuss them as a group. Verbally sharing our thoughts often helps to clarify our own ideas.

I urge you to make a daily To Do List so that by delegating the small things that clutter your mind to paper, you remove them. The To Do List serves as a daily guide to structure your day and provide the most effective use of your hours. The act of writing down your goals serves in an identical manner. When you see on paper the things you want to do in ten years, it provides a visible reminder. The act of writing the words will serve as a promise and as a contract to yourself.

Writing your ten year goals may be easier said than done. Draw a blank? Don't worry—it happens to almost everyone. Here the timer comes to the rescue again. We are pushing the Parkinson Law out of our lives.

Set the timer—begin to write a list of one or two word goals. You may be writing the general goals as everyone does automatically—the way you would answer on a quiz show if you were given ten seconds to make three wishes. Health, Money, Travel—were you thinking of these? One of them? Perhaps you had another list—however, most people do think of these and in that order. Now—that is fine and they may be listed as goals. Each of them will qualify for the subgoals, or the little half steps (as we refer to the steps necessary to achieve a given goal)—and go ahead and put these on the paper. Be sure to cover the career goals.

Are you working now?

Do you like your career—or is it simply a job? If your answer is job—start thinking in terms of a career.

An interesting article by Carol Kleiman in the Chicago *Tribune,* reported a statement by Marge Rossman, of Women's Inc., a counseling, career planning, management, recruiting, and consultant firm in Hinsdale, Illinois.

"Rossman finds women are sometimes more job-oriented than career-oriented. Basically, a job meets an immediate material goal, such as money for a car, college, or house and may be dropped when the goal is reached, but a career involves growth in skills, knowledge, and responsibility on a consistent basis."

And Paula Nelson, in *The Joy of Money,* explained her start in a very successful business had much to do with goals. "I had targeted my goal, planned how to achieve it—and I had the pleasure of realizing that accomplishment. I look at goals as a kind of personal road map."

The analogy of visualizing a road map helps to put goals into the right perspective—how to get from here to there.

Set the timer for ten minutes and list as many goals as you can. Don't involve yourself in a study of how you might achieve the goals—just write and keep on moving down the page and over to the next side and on until the timer goes off.

Now take the list and look at the things you have listed. This may be the first time you ever put on paper the thoughts of what you would like to do with your life. Isn't it ironic to think we spend hours and hours selecting a certain wardrobe that will serve us for a season, or perhaps a few years—but, a plan that involves our future life doesn't get that much attention?

The importance of this ten-year goal sheet cannot be overemphasized. It is your first step toward achieving the things you want. The clearness of the path to success is outlined by the steppingstones you will use along the way.

Take the ten year goal sheet and select from those categories the three that are most meaningful to you. This choice may be difficult and it may happen that two are closely related to one another. You can select four if they seem realistic—or even six, if this does not cause fragmentation.

Take your choices and work out a realistic checklist of ways you shall attempt to reach the goal.

For instance, a young mother with two preschool children projected her goal sheet with the ages of her children a definite factor in her choice. Because they will be in elementary school for much of that time, she put her first choice, "Owning and operating my own photography studio," as a ten-year goal.

Under her half-steps, she listed community college courses in photography to keep her current. Since she was intensely interested in the field of child photography, she planned to take photos of the children in the nursery and early elementary classes that her own young children would be attending. Her plans went consecutively up the ladder to an obvious record of all homework completed by the time ten years had elasped.

When we introduced the six month goal sheet, the six week, and the weekly goal plan, this same enthusiastic young mother was able to fill the blanks without a moment's hesitation. She was focusing directly toward her "career"—not a job—a career.

Compare her plan with that of a woman who majored in photography and has the credentials necessary for her career. However, if she simply quits to raise children and care for a home and does not establish a goal that provides a continual course toward professional photography, the ten years will slip by and she will not have moved any closer than she was following her graduation. The degrees serve her only if she has a plan to use them.

Six-Month Goals

Set the timer again, this time for six minutes. You will find it is easier now . . . a closer time span makes focusing easier and six-month goals will be a fun exercise. What do you see about the six-month list and the ten-year list? Any repeats? Do you see a relationship between some of the goals?

Perhaps you already have a definite direction and listing this information will simply reinforce your pattern. If you have completed the six month list—take another six minutes on the timer and do a list for:

Six-Week Goals: This further breakdown will help prepare your To Do List. You may have a great number of self-improvement items, improvement of your home or apartment, plans to entertain, trips, and this type of listing on a six-week goal sheet. It is important to again narrow the selection to a few top priorities and concentrate on getting them finished. Alert yourself to the energy channel that can be most effective if it is not fragmented.

If reading about these exercises finds you not wanting to do them, I suggest you put the homework aside for a few days and concentrate on review of the past assignments. Come back to this chapter when you have given some thought to the importance of controlling the direction of your life.

I can fully appreciate anyone's hesitation to fill out charts for the sake of filling out charts. However, in the case of a goal sheet—it does have a lot going for it and often turning the exercise into a game helps. Call a friend to come over and join you. Create a "goal planning party" or come up with your own ideas.

ASSIGNMENT:

Take time for yourself each day

Understand the importance of daydreaming—do it.
Prepare a ten-year goal sheet.

List all the half steps you will use to achieve the goals.

Prepare the six-month and six-week goal sheets.

Keep these visible and update regularly.

Transfer applicable items to your To Do List.

Seven

PREPLANNING AND PRENEED

Great!! The results are felt and you start to recognize the control. However, a top priority to living is that of crises. The home, food, clothing, and routine—all become secondary when death or illness strikes. Preplanning is insurance against the time you will be ill equipped to make rational decisions.

The woman is seated across from her family lawyer of the past ten years. She is in an obvious state of grief, frustration and desperation. Her usual poise and perfect grooming are suffering in the wake of her personal sorrow. Unable to continue her attempt to understand, she lashes out in anger:

"Why didn't you tell me, Stan. I should have known the debts and the mess our financial state was in before now. What can I do with Bob dead, three children to raise, and no income?"

This scene may sound like a soap opera but variations of it are happening daily in all too real life. The woman may be widowed, divorced, or single but the message is the same.

It is time financial incompetence stops being equated with women.

Perhaps we are the victim of a myth, the child primer that showed Father Dick going off to work and Mother Jane staying home in a protective state of unconcern. Childhood experiences have influenced many into believing the world of money is understood only by men. Women often feel intimidated by their weakness in arithmetic. Not all women—but some do find figures difficult. How often have you heard, "Money, oh dear! I can't even balance my own checkbook"? Or—when an organization is looking for a treasurer, "I have always been terrible with figures—you'll have to count me out."

The message I want to share in this chapter is: It is never too early and often too late to look objectively at your entire life and money plays an important role whether we like it or not.

Now is the time to understand the importance of money control. Unless you know exactly what is your financial worth, you are distinctly handicapped. Unless you realize your outstanding debts, you are gambling in a losing battle. Unless you admit to your lack of knowledge, you will be the victim of a great loss.

There are several directions you can follow in your desire to finally understand the meaning of a financial statement. The best way is the easy way.

Enroll in a financial seminar.

This will serve as a stimulus and provide the material you will need for further study. Additionally, excellent reference texts on the market will be recommended and with the course as a guideline, you will be able to draw up a brief but adequate financial report of your worth. The lesson will be complete.

Because husbands often "handle that sort of thing," women frequently enjoy a false security. Such security is dangerous. Take the time now, while your thinking is clear to put your financial affairs in order.

Our students appreciate the simple guide we provide in the class seminars.

This form represents a basic record. Your individual financial statement may be more complex. Fill out this form or one your legal advisor may prepare for you, and keep it continually updated. Good idea to use pencil for this purpose.

ASSETS AND LIABILITIES

Cash	$ _____
Savings Accounts	_____
Mutual Funds	_____
Stocks	_____
Bonds	_____
Life Insurance	_____
Other	_____
Total	$ _____
Outstanding debts	$ _____
Amt. charged on Credit Accounts	_____
Home Mortgage	_____
Misc.	_____
Total	$ _____

Because the subject of death and taxes are often dreaded, it's human to avoid discussing them. However, it is the wise and mature adult who recognizes the importance of preplanning and takes the steps to protect his or her estate from a major shrinkage of assets that can easily happen.

91

Let us examine the word "Estate" a bit. 1) It is defined as "A sizable piece of rural land, usually with a large house," and 2) "The whole of one's possessions, especially all of the property and debts left by a deceased or bankrupt person." Too often estate is equated with great wealth. Actually it means "one's possessions," personal property such as an automobile, clothing, paintings, a stamp collection, and the hundreds of material things you don't think of as representing an "estate."

The term "estate planning" means many things to many people. I have taken the mystery out of the term and explain to my students that it is not a complex program. In brief, estate planning is a plan to conserve your assets.

One works long hours, many days, weeks, years, to build a savings of monies, property, and possessions. If an estate is not protected, one suffers needless losses. Benefits that may have been given to heirs are gulped up by taxes, probate, and fees.

An article appearing in the Dallas *Morning News*, reported by Merle E. Dowd, stated: "As many as 70 percent of decedents die without a proper will and this void forces court disposition of assets according to state laws." Give a moment's thought to the great loss this represents to the heirs of the deceased. A lifetime of working and saving and not a word said about the direction of the estate upon death. It seems foolish for anyone to put off the drawing up of a will; but obviously it is continually put off, delayed, forgotten and suddenly—it is too late!

The important moment to take the step toward planning for the future is NOW. Don't put it off until retirement. You might be one of the twenty-six million retired Americans that Melvin Jay Schwartz, attorney specializing in estate planning, says has been wronged. He refers to the lack of proper advice they have had in planning their retirement. They are the targets of con artists who benefit from their

ignorance. Attorney Schwartz warns that the greatest ᴜᴜ⸝
take is simply not spending a little money for sound, correct
advice. He says, "People will take the word of a supermar-
ket clerk, a bank teller, a friend's cousin, almost anyone
whose information is free—with enormous later costs in
their losses."

The lesson is learned too late—for too many. Don't fall
victim to taking advice from those not trained in the legal
field. You can erase the myth that says planning for the
future is complex—it is an intelligent and essential move
that provides enormous benefits.

Preneed Checklist

Keeping this information all in one place will be of tre-
mendous help to you, your spouse, relative, or whomever
must have the documents at the time of emergency or death
of the owner.

1. Will. If married, both husband and wife should have
   wills. Place them in a safe deposit box and keep a second copy at home. The lawyer who helped you prepare
   the will will also keep a copy.
2. Assets and Liabilities sheet.
3. Legal name and social security number of each family
   member.
4. A list of policy insurance numbers and where the
   policies are located. Note the beneficiaries and coverage
   that each insurance policy provides.
5. List a full account of the stocks, bonds, certificates of
   deposit, real estate holdings, and other assets.
6. List a full account of the liabilities, mortgages, and
   taxes.
7. Original or photostat copies of all family records. Birth
   certificates, Marriage, Death, Military, etc.

Elizabeth M. Fowler, *New York Times* financial colum-
nist, has written a financial primer. She explains: "All married women should prepare themselves to be widows, no
matter what their age or their status in life." Her book by
Little, Brown is titled: *How to Manage Your Money: A
Woman's Guide to Investing.* An excellent paperback
which helps to explain the fact half the widows over 65
today live on less than $2000 a year is *You and Your Pen-
sion.* It was compiled by Ralph Nader and Kate Blackwell.
Lynn Caine, author of the best seller, *Widow,* proposes an
annual review of the financial status of your family. She
calls it "Contingency Day." The day should reflect love,
caring and responsibility—plus common sense, she says;
and suggests the day's agenda should include consideration
of steps to be taken if either husband or wife should die in
the next twelve months, 2) how much money the surviving
spouse and children have to live on, and 3) what changes in
lifestyle will be necessary.

The all important question is the amount needed to live
and to support the family. To regularly establish a yearly
review is a mature action. Unfortunately, most people
procrastinate and avoid setting up such a plan because of
what Caine calls a "Strong Death Taboo" which prevents
us from dealing with the inevitability of death.

Sometimes a point is driven home when a true life story
of another's grief is told. The newspaper account of a traffic
killing, the grief stricken father and his three young children
are pictured staring from the pages of your morning newspaper as the photograph shows the crumpled auto that took
the life of the mother. The agony and loss felt by this young
family becomes even more difficult if financial need is an
additional problem.

The young father is faced with the immediate need of
hiring someone to come and care for the children. This is
not an easy bill to fill and often times there is a rude awaken-

ing when one learns the amount of money that must be paid for domestic chores and child rearing duties. It can be a tragic truth that only in loss is the monetary worth of the woman's role understood and appreciated.

Let us assume this young family started their marriage with a solid investment of professional help. They had occasion to witness very early in their life the importance of adequate insurance protection, of estate planning and in quick summary—of preparing for a crisis.

The crisis occurs: A phone call to alert the insurance agent, the lawyer, and the next of kin.

Results: An automatic transfer of the responsibilities, pressures and details that demand attention are handled by the competent advisors they selected.

The emotional instability that every human experiences at the time of personal loss is a dangerous climate in which to make decisions. The time for decisions is *NOW*—this very day.

Never Too Early and Often Too Late

Let us assume the checklist and records have been supplied. Now we will take a clear look at the action one must take regarding funeral arrangements. Seldom is there any discussion about how to dispose of one's body before death. It again goes back to the "Strong Death Taboo" and realistically, we will act on the premise that most people die without specific instruction.

A San Francisco *Chronicle* report on June 25, 1974, by reporter Barbara Falconer, explains:

"The legal right—and duty—to control the final disposition of a body goes to the deceased's spouse, children, parents, and other relatives in that order.

"If both the deceased and his survivors, if any, are indigent the county will take over the burial and the expense. In this case, the relatives have to sign social security and other benefits over to the county."

Included in the same article was this vital information regarding *"THE RED TAPE"* of dying. Two documents, a Certificate of Death and a Permit for Disposition of Human Remains, are required. The attending physician or the coroner must fill out the medical certification on the death certificate, which must then be filed with the local registry of births and deaths.

The registry issues the disposition permit to the funeral director, or you, if you are acting as funeral director yourself. On the permit, you must specify either the place the remains are to be buried or entombed, or the crematory and the final destination of the ashes.

It is wise to obtain several certified copies of the death certificate at the time of filing. They are necessary when applying for social security and other benefits.

Read the last sentence in the previous paragraph again. "They are necessary when applying for social security and other benefits."

Thousands of people neglect to apply for benefits that are due them. In some cases, social security payments may be one's only source of income.

Take the following papers with you when you go to the nearest Social Security office to apply:
1. Death certificate
2. Marriage license
3. Social Security numbers; yours and his.
4. Children's birth certificates
5. Proof of age. Your birth certificate or driver's license.

Because the processing of your claim will take time, you may not receive your first check for several months. The checks will be retroactive and all Social Security and the Veterans Administration benefits are tax-exempt.

Too often we equate social security benefits with death. There are many benefits in the program of social security and your local office can give you full information. Give them a call today.

Martha Yates relates her own moving and painful experience of widowhood in an excellent book entitled, *Coping.* It is a survival manual for women alone and is packed with vital information that every woman should read. Ms. Yates explains there are more than fifteen million single, widowed, or divorced women in the United States today.

She provides a wealth of personal insight and practical suggestions based on her experience and how she learned to cope with her radically changed life as a widow.

This piece of information was brand new to me and I want to share it. On page 53 of her book, she explains:

"If you are a widow and are afraid that you may overlook some benefits to which you may be entitled, good news. There is a free service provided by 381 banks in 30 states that will help you search out and claim all financial benefits that may be due you. These could be through retirement funds, union and other pensions, profit-sharing plans, credit life insurance, workmen's compensation, and others. You don't have to be a customer of one of the member banks to avail yourself of this service; write for a national directory of the banks to: Special Organizational Services, P.O. Box S.O.S., Athens, Texas 75751."

In preparing the material included in this chapter, I digested volumes on the subject of taxes, estate planning, insurance programs, and wills. The list is fully covered in the Bibliography and I encourage you to read any or all of the texts. Additionally, talk with estate lawyers, trust department employees of banks, and a funeral director. My research resulted in statistics, suggestions, and pages of notes. Because I want this book to translate the message into human terms, I have pared away the complex and strived for simplicity. The information is intended to serve as a guide but never as a substitute for legal advice. Hopefully, the charts will be filled out and the checklist completed as your homework assignment for this chapter.

It is a sobering truth that a fraction of one's time given toward a program of preplanning and preneed can save a lifetime of assets from being lost to poor management.

Keep in mind *Estate Planning* is not only for the wealthy. It is even more important to the small estate. Here is why! Because of the fact there is limited income—there is no margin for loss due to unnecessary taxes, neglect, or error. A will is the cornerstone of planning. Do not procrastinate another day if you do not have a will. Wills are not expensive and it is equally important that they are reviewed and kept updated.

ASSIGNMENT:

ASSETS AND LIABILITIES—Copy or type the basic outline and fill in the information. Use pencil to allow for corrections.

PRENEED CHECKLIST—Make a will. Consult a lawyer if you do not have one at this time. Sound legal advice can save you hundreds of dollars and is just as important as a good insurance advisor. This team is exceedingly important in time of crisis.

ESTABLISH A "CONTINGENCY DAY"—Lynn Caine's message is clear and simple. Her best seller, WIDOW, explains the Contingency Day and she gives excellent support for establishing this annual day of re-evaluation. I urge you to pick up a copy of her book. Available in hardback, paperback and libraries.

Eight

HALF STEPS

For those of you who have your lives firmly in "control" and have progressed to having "time for yourself," now you will want to explore further who you are and what you are *really* like. The seeking of identity is both the problem and the solution.

"A journey of ten thousand miles begins with but a single step." Chinese Proverb

That first, single step is often the most difficult to take— but, be assured, half steps are fifty percent easier than full steps. You may already be taking half steps in a subconscious aim toward a future full step.

Time is what it's all about. For some, time falls heavy and it is the same problem in reverse for those who never have enough time. Whatever your status in life at this particular moment, I encourage you to take conscious control of your days—and your life. Everyone can take daily half steps that will provide direction toward a rewarding goal.

Tish Baldrige in her super book, *Juggling,* speaks about the working woman. "To manage, you do have to master the fine art of juggling. Any juggling, . . . means making every moment count." She explains she loves her work, but does not love her children any less for it. "If I were home all day, playing an active role in the children's lives, I would release all my pent-up frustrations on them. The children sense this. We even talk about it. They also know, however, that when the red trouble flag is up, I'll be there."

Many women I interviewed shared this same feeling about their children. They need the time away and when forced to remain home all of the time their "pent-up frustrations" overflowed. It is a human trait and although there are exceptions, many women are eager to find a challenging and profitable activity. The degree of "eagerness" determined the direction they were taking, and the amount of time they were willing to spend away from the family. Many have taken half steps which provide the interest and release they desire, but which can be almost totally accomplished at home.

As you read newspapers and magazines stay constantly alert for articles that pique your interest. You will find a wealth of information on current interests which result in creating a demand and that is where you, yes, you personally, step in and help meet the supply. Your unique creativity could well plunge you into new, exciting and successful ventures you never dreamed possible.

A word of caution, however; be alert to organizations or individuals who set up "work at home" schemes that yearly exploit tens of thousands of women who are looking for ways to make money at home. Before you make any decisions to participate in any way check it out with your Better Business Bureau or seek expert advice from your attorney, bank, or other professional whom you trust.

The secret is in doing; not talking, not wishing, not dreaming, but doing. Come along. Play this paper game and see if it reveals any secrets. Undoubtedly it will jog some hidden ambitions, talents—interests.

For the purposes of exploration and to keep things in an orderly manner, we will borrow from the alphabet and let the letters serve as a guide to help stimulate the imagination:

Art? Antiques? Alterations?

Art: Interested in art? Previous training, degrees, job experience? Perhaps not, but it doesn't exclude you from exploring the field. Docent programs are available at many museums. Art appreciation courses are offered and home correspondence courses are possible if you possess disciplined study habits. Get to know the owners of art galleries; consider volunteering your time a few hours a week. Try your hand at painting; a hobby or a career may be the result. Exploring the field of art may open a new dimension to your life. Continual exposure to the opportunities in the field may result in art investment for profit.

Antiques: Adore antiques? Perhaps a mixture of new and old? Anyone furnishing a home, apartment, flat, or mansion, has spent time looking for furnishings. Not all antiques are resting on expensive Oriental rugs and closeted within the walls of a prestigious collector's shop. Try the fun of scouting garage sales, second-hand shops, estate sales and auctions. An enterprising college art student on the East Coast invited a friend to join him on weekends clearing and cleaning garages and attics in a rural area of New England. They did a good job; charged a fair price, and were able to purchase antiques from owners willing and often anxious to sell.

The two have just opened their second antique store and used the half steps during those college weekends to prepare for the goal of their own business.

Alterations: Enjoy sewing? Perhaps clothing—but, not necessarily so. Alterations can mean a hemline change or a closet converted into a dark room. It may mean transforming a run-down piece of property into a profitable sale because of alterations. A friend built a lucrative business in a few short years by perfecting alterations she knew were necessary to restore famed Victorian homes in San Francisco.

The term alterations opens the door to a wide range of business possibilities. A small "at home alteration service" can grow into a sewing school, or a studio of fashion design A creative talent can be pursued with half steps of study, practice, and perseverance.

Baking? Boutiques? Banking?

Baking: Every Christmas, several of my friends receive a Miss Grace Lemon Cake mailed from Beverly Hills, California. The cake is delicious and within each tin is a brochure telling how Miss Grace started baking her first lemon cakes for friends and the business grew because of quality and demand. Many excellent bakery products which enjoy national distribution today started in the kitchen of some enterprising cook.

A more realistic half step might be in providing "Specialty Cakes" for birthdays or other occasions. A supply of business cards passed out to friends and neighbors would probably provide a market. A small ad in your local paper would be justified when business is slow.

Boutiques: A successful boutique requires hard work, long hours, and an understanding of the market. Too often, the homework is forgotten when riding on the wave of enthusiasm for a new idea. Research, review the kind of boutique and potential market in the location you want. For every boutique that may fail, one may thrive—yours could be that one. A unique quality business started by two capable women in Dallas, Texas, was patterned after a favorite boutique they liked in New York. Imagination helped to launch their career, in addition to a policy of free alterations and gift wrapping. Now, a Silver Cloud Rolls-Royce is used in making deliveries and transporting special customers.

Talent, creativity, ambition, and hard work are some of the ingredients necessary. If you are not free for such an ambitious undertaking now—but, a friend or neighbor owns one, ask them the pro's and the con's of such a business. Volunteer some time and the experience will tell you if retail merchandising is enjoyable.

Banking: More and more opportunities are available in the field of banking for women today. If it intrigues you, pursue the study that will be necessary. The women I interviewed in banking agreed it takes education, patience, hard work, and long hours. You can stimulate your interest in a variety of ways. Working in a bank is obviously a help up the ladder. However, if you must stay home, use these years to become an expert in a specialized field of banking service. Attend seminars in financial planning, enroll in a course in estate planning. Read, study, ask questions of the experts in the field. The awareness of what is available is your first step in learning if you might be interested.

Cooking? Catering? Calisthenics?

You may have a completely different listing for the "C" category. If you are a gourmet cook, the opportunity for a business may be in your kitchen. A couple of ambitious, alert young women in Long Island decided there was a market for casseroles and quiche to sell to people returning from the beach. They set up shop in a rural section of Long Island between Southampton and East Hampton and enjoyed instant success.

Fast food outlets are taking over everywhere. The need for specialized food, prepared well and delivered is in demand.

Catering: Perhaps your area is ripe for catered children's parties. With imagination, realistic prices and a few party favors, a thriving business could be developed on a shoe string. Catering opportunities are everywhere—create some half steps today and learn the potential in your area.

Calisthenics: Start an exercise class in your recreation room. If teaching appeals to you, a sense of body fitness is part of your life, and a business opportunity is born. Exercise classes, controlled diet, a program of calisthenics—whatever you want to include. Obviously, this instruction takes knowledge, education, and enthusiasm. The benefits are personal. You keep physically fit because of a regular program of teaching those in your class the benefits of exercise through calisthenics.

Dress Design? Drafting? Distributor?

The 'D' list can encompass hundreds of opportunities. The dress design business is not for the novice; however, working one's way into this field can prove exciting and rewarding. Fashion illustration is taught in home correspondence courses, at schools and colleges. Serving as an apprentice is an ideal method of learning the trade. Awareness of design and current trends in the field of fashion will be the first indication of your potential.

104

Drafting: A girlfriend I met years ago in Kansas City has successfully combined a drafting career and motherhood. She married in the late 50's, had three children in the same number of years, followed them through the stages of nursery, early elementary, Girl Scouts, cub scouts, camping trips, dance classes, basketball, football, and finally highschool. Her father was a draftsman and she often dropped by his office to help with the clerical duties. One year one of his draftsmen was gone for an entire summer and he asked her to fill in. The assignment was exciting and she asked for others. She spent every free hour at his office and today has her own firm and directs several employees.

Sound interesting?—explore the possibilities.

Distributor: One can be a distributor of cosmetics, clothing, shoes, food, furniture—the list is endless. Usually defined as a wholesaler, the field is wide open for women but the ability to travel may be a prerequisite. Others called home distributors use the "party plan" to sell products. The dealer demonstrates the houseware, jewelry, cosmetic, whatever the product, and the guests may order on the spot. Some distributors are extremely successful. This appeals to some but not to others. Consider keeping the category "distributor" on your personal list. It involves many choices.

Now you have the idea—continue and consider your personal list. Some additional random categories you may wish to give some thought include:

E——Exercise and the specialized business involving exercise for animals including walking dogs regularly. Many are well able to afford such a service and would welcome a business that offers morning and afternoon outings for their pampered pets. These same customers often travel and would be grateful for the services of a "Professional Pet Sitter"—a lucrative business for those who enjoy animals.

F——*Framing* is a field that can be started on small scale. One's own garage, rec room, or small studio may prove adequate to try your skill in "framing." In fact "Do It Yourself" frame stores are popping up many places. Working with a craftsman who has had years of experience in the field is the fastest way of learning the work, so do make an effort to visit one of these if framing interests you.

Free-lancing: An ideal way to gain experience, and an opportunity to learn what really holds your interest. You may need additional education or experience to pursue part-time work as a free-lance photographer, copy editor, professional book indexer, or model. Signing up with an agency which provides temporary jobs may open doors to various possible avenues of interest by placing you in clerical positions in different fields. Or, call a modeling agency which contracts for adults and children. Other family members may be included in your half steps and this could lead you on an exciting and profitable venture together. Parents frequently find that acting as agent for a photogenic family member is a full-time effort and a lucrative one.

G——*Gardening?* Anyone with a green thumb can find profit with a little imagination, advertising and ambition. There are baby sitters, pet sitters, and plant sitters. People who travel are eager to have their plants tended. A few satisfied customers readily tell others about your business and, again, the small half steps taken during a period in one's life when a side interest provides good balance, lays the foundation for a full career later.

G——Gourmet and Groceries. This brings to mind cooking classes, a special collection of gourmet recipes, bound attractively and perhaps included in gift food packages. What's your specialty? It might be a jar of curried mayonnaise, special mustard sauce, or perhaps a homemade paté, together with your booklet of recipes nestled in a gingham-lined berry basket.

A couple of years ago, a visitor from the rural area of Maryland explained her specialized gourmet selections were sold directly from her home. Her clients were willing to make the distant trip to her home and select the attractive food packages. She did not have delivery or mail service because it was her intention to control the size during the years her children needed her at home. However, she is planning on future expansion and these early years are half steps to assure the success and her enjoyment of full-time business later.

H——Hats, Horses, and Housekeeping. The making and selling of various types and styles of hats. Training, caring, and raising of horses. Housekeeping turned to profit? Jeanine Duffy of Memphis trains housekeepers for all the Holiday Inns.

*I——*What does your list include for the letter "I?" A good insurance agent is a friend to clients and offers an all important service. A variety of types and categories are available. Start by investigating the opportunities in your area. Talk to those who are successful in the field of selling insurance. Explore if this is an area you would find interesting and stimulating.

Other listings for "I"—Inventor, Investigator.

J——Jewelry? Here is a success story you may have read about in the August 1976 *Harper's Bazaar.* Francene Tolken and Barbara Hirsch are both in their mid-thirties, married and each have three children. Friends since the second grade they dabbled in making jewelry. Today, they run a $250,000 jewelry firm called AIZ—complete with factory and two showrooms, in Los Angeles and another in New York.

When interviewed, they explained: "The business started by mistake." It seemed they wore their own jewelry and people would ask to buy it. Store buyers even began to ask about it and place orders. Starting on a small scale, they later hired employees and their husbands contributed in business decisions and with design, packaging and advertising.

Their advice to anyone wanting to start a business: "Work with someone you respect and admire who will listen and relate to you. Surround yourself with the best possible creative thinkers. Stay open to all suggestions. Share ideas generously—you will get many back. Don't be afraid to risk rejection."

Additional categories include Journalist, Jobber and many other possibilities. Any interest?

K——*Kathy's Koffee Klatch.* This small meeting place in southern Minnesota supported a family of six growing boys and financed their education. Kathy, a strong and determined woman of Swedish ancestry, lost her husband in the early 50's. Her formal education had been limited and she reached back to her skill in baking to start a business that provided financial security during some rough years. Her small, crowded diner served the finest pies and cakes for miles around. She purposely kept the menu small and controlled the business so it never grew out of her ability to manage. As the children grew, they helped some; however,

Kathy prided herself in handling every detail. A delicious cup of freshly brewed coffee, piece of homemade pie, and lots of conversation. That formula put Kathy's Koffee Klatch on the map.

Kindergarten is another possible category for those who enjoy teaching and youngsters.

M——Message? Manners? Mailing? Manicures? The list is endless. Marriage and motherhood may be the space you are in at this time. If your responsibilities control your mobility, you may be interested in the "M" categories mentioned above.

Message refers to an answering service, and depending upon your area, this is sometimes combined with a direct mail service. Prerequisite necessary: Ability to type if interested in direct mail business. The stuffing of envelopes and mailing literature during political campaigns, bond issues, and other mass mailings may be a repetitive task; but provides experience in many areas and offers exposure to fields you may want to pursue.

N——Nursing can be a full-time career or a part-time vocation. Many trained nurses will pick up their careers after ten or fifteen years of child rearing. There are varied opportunities for women with a degree in nursing. With additional administrative training, careers never dreamed of by women of past generations are opening in hospital administration and related fields.

Jotting down thoughts about the letter "O," my first thought, personally, is of course: Organizer. This category appeared years ago on a similar paper exercise in which I participated. What "O" subjects are yours?

P——Plants? Painting? Parties? Relate the one word subject into areas of half steps that may work for you. Each category can mean meeting new and interesting people and learning from them. Go on through the alphabet and let your imagination be your guide.

Some of our subjects may require more research or additional school; but many require only your interest and a desire to try. One of the most important factors which will contribute greatly to your success is *your* attitude. It can, in fact, make the crucial difference between success and failure. Just as you assumed the title and acted the part of executive in taking over control of your home office, you must also approach either a mini-career or a major career with a positive and professional attitude.

A professional is frequently nothing more than an ambitious amateur—the true test of reaching professional staus is believing in yourself. You must take yourself seriously if you expect others to take you seriously.

Women have been said to *fear* success; but I haven't met those women. Success is *Super Fun*!

ASSIGNMENT

Prepare a list of the "half steps" you can do to prepare for the time you can take a full step. Magazines and books are excellent sources to stimulate your ideas.

Check your goal sheet and enter subgoals. The half steps will assure your attaining them.

Turn a hobby into a free-lance career. The areas are many and growing each year. Remember the help a business card gives you. Often it tells you who you are and that can be a first step toward moving forward.

Half steps are simply a disciplined use of one's blocks of time on a regular routine of charting a path that directs your life to where *you* want to be.

Start now to use this book as a friend. It will serve as a guide, a teacher and a test. Keep it handy and follow step by step until all homework assignments have been completed.

You will notice the results immediately. When your life starts to have direction and you sense a control that you have been missing—the feeling will be that of "winning" and you are the winner.

RESOURCES

I have researched extensively for a listing of classes that might be available in personal time management for women. Hundreds of replies were received answering my request for information, but the area of time management for women remains elusive. However, many programs are available for women in counseling, career aids, resume guidance, job referral, placement and a variety of topics.

Because new programs are continually being formed, I suggest you do some individual research in your local area. The wealth of material available from the following organizations is yours for the asking. Do go to your local Yellow Pages and check any listing for: Women's Resource Center or Women's Counseling Center.

To help focus the listing, I will put the names in alphabetical order. Drop a card to those you are interested in and telephone any listings in your local area.

ADULT EDUCATION CENTERS: Frequently, career clinics and job preparation workshops are part of the programs offered.

ADVOCATES FOR WOMEN, INC.: 593 Market St., Suite 500, San Francisco, Cal. 94105. Career counseling, job referral, placement.

ALMANAC: The Women's Almanac is a magazine published by the Armitage Press, Inc., 1430 Massachusetts Ave., Cambridge, Mass. 02138. Copies may be ordered by writing to the publisher.

BALTIMORE NEW DIRECTIONS FOR WOMEN: 1100 E. Eutaw St., Baltimore, Md. 21201. Government agency.

BOSTON PROJECT FOR CAREERS: 83 Prospect St., West Newton, Mass. 02165. Educational and career counseling, job referral, placement (especially part time).

CATALYST: A national nonprofit organization, headquartered in New York City. Provides services to meet the needs of women in various stages of career development. Currently, a network of 150 resource centers are available. A series of Career Option booklets has been recently released which stress opportunities in ten nontraditional fields in which Catalyst says there are many shortages of women. These fields are: accounting, banking, engineering, finance, government and politics, industrial management, insurance, retail management, restaurant management and sales. For information on Catalyst's services, write: Catalyst, 6 East 82nd St., New York, N.Y. 10028.

CONTINUING EDUCATION COURSES FOR WOMEN: *The New York Times Guide to Continuing Education in America.* Available from publisher, write to the following: Quadrangle Books, 10 East 53rd St., New York, N.Y. 10017.

U.S. Department of Labor: *Continuing Education Programs and Services for Women.* Write: Superintendent of Documents, GPO, Washington, D.C. 20402

Directory of Counseling Services. Write publisher: International Association of Counseling Services, Inc., 1607 New Hampshire Ave. N.W., Washington, D.C. 20009.

C.R.I.S.P. (Consumer Resource Information Service Program): Information to help housewives utilize their food dollars, improve home management; the focus is directed toward saving time and money. For more information, write: CRISP Building, 1221 S. Brookhurst, Anaheim, Cal. 92804.

DISTAFFERS RESEARCH AND COUNSELING CENTER: Provides private counseling and workshops. Write: 4625a 41 St. N.W., Washington D.C. 20016.

DYNAMICS OF SELF-ORGANIZATION AND PERSONALITY ASSESSMENT: A seven-week course offered at Denver Free University and taught by Roger Fuehrer. For additional information: Denver Free University, 1122 East 17th Ave., P.O. Box 18455, Denver, Colo. 80218.

EFFECTIVE FEEDBACK INC.: Provides personal planning workshops. An area is directed toward time management. Write: 840 Brookwood Place, Ann Arbor, Mich. 48104.

EXECUTIVE ENTERPRISES, THE DISTAFF GROUP: Publishes a full list of the seminars for women planned in ten major cities throughout the United States. Focus is toward the businesswoman who lacks formal instruction in finance. Courses include "Fundamentals of Finance" and "Principles of Supervisory Management for the Newly Promoted Woman." Write: 10 Columbus Circle, New York, N.Y. 10019.

FEMINIST JOB COUNSELING: For information, write: Options: Career Workshops for Women, 333 Central Park West, New York, N.Y. 10025.

FLEXIBLE CAREERS: A skills registry for ready-to-work, qualified applicants wishing part-time or flexi-time jobs. Contact: Flexible Careers, YWCA, 37 S. Wabash, Chicago, Illinois.

INDIVIDUAL DEVELOPMENT CENTER: An independent private agency focusing on career and life decision counseling. Career development workshops for company and government agency employees, awareness seminars for managers and supervisors of women employees. For information: Individual Development Center, Inc., 1020 E. John St., Seattle, Wash. 98102.

JOB SEARCH: Placement assistance for job hunters who are seeking jobs traditionally reserved for men. Write to: Job Search, Women's Resource Center, YWCA, 1111 S.W. 10th St., Portland, Ore. 97205.

LEADERSHIP AND TRAINING TASK FORCE: Teaches skills necessary to realize one's career goals. Write to: Judith Geschwind, 2306 Greenery Lane, Silver Springs, Md. 20906.

MORE FOR WOMEN: This program provides career reorientation in two parts. The first is assessment of off- and on-the-job skills and the second a job search and review of options. Write: More for Women, 2 Lexington Ave., New York, N.Y. 10010.

NEW ENVIRONMENTS FOR WOMEN: A career development program focusing on the dynamics of personal growth in a group work situation. Write to: New Environments for Women, 44 Bertwell Road, Lexington, Mass. 02173.

NOW: The National Organization for Women provides a talent bank for all management levels. Write to: NOW, Box 176, Merrick, N.Y. 11566.

OPTIONS FOR WOMEN: A professional staff helps define goals, reorder priorities and explore work opportunities. Write to: Options for Women, 8419 Germantown Ave., Philadelphia, Pa. 19118.

ORGANIZATION PLUS: Stella O'Brien founded this business. Home management and space organization are highlighted. For information, write to: Stella O'Brien, 1330 Rosemary, Denver, Colo.

PROFESSIONAL SCHOOLS AND ASSOCIATIONS that are listed in your Yellow Pages may help in your search for the program you desire. Check your phone directory.

WOMANSCHOOL: Founded to help women learn basic skills, knowledge and acquire self-confidence to improve their life situations and to adjust to the changing female role. This adult education center, founded in spring of 1975, is the one single school aimed at the practical needs of women forced by today's cultural dynamics to re-evaluate and restructure their thinking, actions, and lifestyles. Write to: Adult Education Center Inc., 170 East 70th St., New York, N.Y. 10021.

WOMEN'S CENTER: Write to: Orange Coast College, 2701 Fairview Road, Costa Mesa, Cal. 92626.

WOMEN'S OPPORTUNITIES CENTER: Write the University of California, Irvine, Cal. 92664.

WOMEN'S YELLOW PAGES: Original source book for women; appeared first in Boston 1972 and again in 1974. Direct your inquiry to: Boston Women's Collective Inc., 490 Beacon St., Boston, Mass. 02115.

BIBLIOGRAPHY

Alter, Jo Anne. "Little Known Ways You Can Earn Extra Money at Home." *Family Circle,* April 1976.

Bacharach, Bert. *How to Do Almost Everything.* New York: Simon & Schuster, Inc., 1970. Paperback: New York: Popular Library, Inc., 1975.

Baldrige, Letitia. *Juggling: The Art of Balancing Marriage, Motherhood, and Career.* New York: The Viking Press, Inc. 1976.

Bloom, Murray Teigh. "What Makes a Successful Family." *Reader's Digest,* May 1973.

Burton, Gabrielle. *I'm Running Away from Home, but I'm Not Allowed to Cross the Street: A Primer on Women's Liberation.* Paperback: New York: Avon Books, 1975.

Caine, Lynn. *Widow.* New York: William Morrow & Co., Inc., 1974. Paperback: New York: Bantam Books, Inc., 1975.

Callahan, Sidney C. *Working Mother: How Liberated Women Can Combine Work with Child Rearing.* New York: Macmillan Publishing Co., Inc., 1971.

Carnegie, Dale. *How to Stop Worrying & Start Living.* New York: Simon & Schuster, 1948. Paperback: Pocket Books, Inc., 1974.

Carnegie, Dale. *How to Win Friends & Influence People.* New York: Simon & Schuster, 1936. Paperback: New York: Pocket Books, Inc., 1975.

Decker, Beatrice, and Kooiman, Gladys. *After the Flowers Have Gone.* Grand Rapids, Michigan: Zondervan Publishing House, 1973.

DeVos, Richard M., and Conn, Charles P. *Believe!* Old Tappan, New Jersey: Fleming H. Revell Co., 1975.

Epstein, Cynthia F. *Woman's Place: Options & Limits in Professional Careers.* Berkeley, California: University of California Press, 1970.

Fensterheim, Herbert, and Baer, Jean. *Don't Say Yes When You Want to Say No.* Paperback: New York Dell Publishing Co., Inc., 1975.

Gilbreth, Lillian M. *Management in the Home: Happier Living Through Saving Time & Energy.* New York: Dodd, Mead & Co., 1959.

Gordon, George Byron. *You, Your Heirs & Your Estate.* Rockville Center, New York: Farnsworth Publishing Co., Inc., 1973.

Habeeb, Virginia T. *The Ladies' Home Journal of Homemaking: Everything You Need to Know to Run Your Home with Ease and Style.* New York: Simon & Schuster, Inc., 1973.

Heloise. *Heloise's Kitchen Hints.* Paperback: New York: Pocket Books, Inc., n.d.

Heloise. *Heloise's Housekeeping Hints.* Paperback: New York: Pocket Books, Inc., n.d.

Hill, Reuben. *Family Development in Three Generations.* Cambridge, Massachusetts: Schenkman Publishing Co., Inc., 1971.

James, Muriel, and Jongeward, Dorothy. *Born to Win: Transactional Analysis with Gestalt Experiments.* Reading, Massachusetts: Addison-Wesley Publishing Co., Inc., 1971.

James, William. "Making Habits Work for You." *Reader's Digest,* August 1967.

Laird, Jean E. *Around the House Like Magic.* Paperback: New York: Tower Publications, Inc., 1971.

Lakein, Alan. *How to Get Control of Your Time & Your Life.* New York: Peter A. Wyden, 1973.

Lembeck, Ruth. *Job Ideas for Today's Woman.* Englewood Cliffs, New Jersey: Prentice-Hall, Inc., 1974.

Lembeck, Ruth. *380 Part-Time Jobs for Women.* Paperback: New York: Dell Publishing Co., Inc., 1968.

Linder, Staffan B. *Harried Leisure Class.* Paperback: New York: Columbia University Press, 1970.

McCay, James T. *Management of Time.* Englewood Cliffs, New Jersey: Prentice-Hall, Inc., 1959.

MacKenzie, R. Alec. *The Time Trap.* Paperback: New York: McGraw-Hill Book Co., 1975.

Miller, Ella M. *Hints for Homemakers.* New Canaan, Connecticut: Keats Publishing, Inc., 1973. Paperback: Scottsdale, Pennsylvania: Herald Press, 1973.

Morse, Theresa A. *Never in the Kitchen When Company Arrives.* New York: Doubleday & Co., Inc., 1964.

Nader, Ralph and Blackwell, Kate. *You and Your Pension.* New York: Grossman, 1972.

Nash, Kathrine. *Get the Best of Yourself: How to Discover Your Success Pattern and Make It Work for You.* New York: Grosset & Dunlap, Inc., 1976.

Nelson, Paula. *The Joy of Money: A Contemporary Woman's Guide to Financial Freedom.* Briarcliff Manor, New York:

Stein & Day, 1975. Paperback: New York: Bantam Books, Inc., 1977.

Oates, Wayne E. *Confessions of a Workaholic.* Paperback: Nashville, Tennessee: 1972, Abingdon Press.

Parkes, Colin M. *Bereavement: Studies of Grief in Adult Life.* New York: International Universities Press, Inc., 1973.

Pogrebin, Letty Cottin. *Getting Yours.* David McKay Co., Inc., 1975. Paperback: New York: Avon Books, 1976.

Seaver, Jeannette. *Jeannette's Secrets of Everyday Good Cooking,* New York: Alfred A. Knopf, Inc., 1975. Paperback: New York: Bantam Books, Inc., 1976.

Stout, Ruth. *It's a Woman's World.* New York: Cornerstone Library Publications, Simon & Schuster, Inc., 1970.

Towle, Charlotte. *Common Human Needs.* Paperback: New York: National Association of Social Workers, 1965.

Trickett, Joseph M. "A More Effective Use of Time." *The California Management Review,* Summer 1962.

Uris, Auren. *Executive Housekeeping: The Business of Managing Your Home.* New York: William Morrow & Co., Inc., 1976.

Whiteside, Lynn. *Know & Do Manager.* Englewood Cliffs, New Jersey: Prentice-Hall, Inc., 1966.

Yates, Martha. *Coping: A Survival Manual for Women Alone.* Englewood Cliffs, New Jersey: Prentice-Hall, Inc., 1976.

Photo by *Martha Brigham*

Donna Goldfein is the founder of ESTE (Easy Steps Toward Efficiency) a popular time-management course in which she conducts classes and seminar/workshops throughout the San Francisco Bay Area. A Management Specialist with American Airlines, she also does public relations work for her husband's corporation. This is in addition to what Donna considers her most important priorities, husband Danny and their three children.

A former Miss Missouri, Donna worked as a freelance model and taught business and communication courses upon graduation from college. Later, while traveling throughout the world in her role with the airlines, she lived in Europe and the Middle East prior to her marriage in 1960. Active in the community, she is

123

presently involved with boards of Church School, Town School Mother's Club, San Francisco Women's Breakfast Club, Youth Guidance Volunteer Auxiliary, Variety Club and National Parliamentarians.

Donna attributes her organizational skills to productive habits learned early and practiced regularly. Her experience as teacher, secretary and airline stewardess provided a system of procedures that she applied to her personal life and now shares regularly with her students during their classes in personal time management.

BOOKS OF RELATED INTEREST

IT'S UP TO YOU is Eileen D. Gambrill and Cheryl A. Richey's basic handbook for developing assertive social skills. Particular attention is devoted to basics: where to go to meet people, handling conversations, arranging meetings, evaluating contacts and making positive changes. 156 pages, soft cover, $4.95

The affirmations set forth in I DESERVE LOVE give you the power to achieve whatever goals you pursue. Defining an affirmation as a positive thought that you choose to immerse in your consciousness to produce a desired result, Sondra Ray presents specific exercises in a variety of areas, including sex, love, self-esteem, affection, and trust to name a few. 128 pages, soft cover, $3.95

Far from being limited to women, the Equal Rights Amendment (ERA) will dramatically affect 100% of the population, both directly and indirectly. IMPACT ERA is the first and only book to predict ways in which the ERA will affect individual rights, employment, education and domestic relations, both legally and socially. Edited by the California Commission on the Status of Women. 288 pages, soft cover, $4.95

CRIMES AGAINST WOMEN documents the shocking testimony heard by the International Tribunal on Crimes Against Women held in Brussels in March, 1976. Diana E.H. Russell and Nicole Van de Ven brilliantly recreate the incidents, record the moving personal accounts of appalling physical and mental brutality, discuss the resolutions and proposals for change, analyze the media's response, and assess the impact of those five incredible days when international feminism was born. 320 pages, soft cover, $5.95

If nothing else is ever written about the pain and joy of being female, Elizabeth Avakian's TO DELIVER ME OF MY DREAMS will serve to tell the story. "It takes time and energy to stay in touch with all my parts and with someone else as well, but for me, at least, the two seem to nourish each other, as long as I feel free to be all the different people I discover I am." 96 pages, soft cover, $3.95

Barbara Kraft explores the anguish of divided loyalties and lost self in her intimate journal, THE RESTLESS SPIRIT: JOURNAL OF A GEMINI. Preface by Anais Nin. 228 pages, soft cover, $4.95

LES FEMMES
Millbrae, California

EVERYWOMAN'S GUIDE SERIES

The immediate success of EVERYWOMAN'S GUIDE TO COLLEGE
clearly illustrated the demand for information by women who are
re-entering society at every level. We are attempting to meet that need
with a major, continuing series of books modeled on the GUIDE TO
COLLEGE format. These are books on

> SUBJECTS THAT ARE TIMELY, of particular concern to
> women, about which information is not readily available
> elsewhere, that provide
> COMPREHENSIVE COVERAGE, with emphasis on practical,
> useful, widely applicable or adaptable information, with
> SOURCES OF ADDITIONAL INFORMATION in a separate
> chapter listing relevant publications, courses, organizations and
> knowledgeable people, and they are
> REASONABLY PRICED so that every woman can afford them.

EVERYWOMAN'S GUIDE TO COLLEGE
Eileen Gray
176 pages $3.95

A logical, no-nonsense study of the emotional, financial and academic
realities of the returning woman student of any age. It includes sections
on how to finance yourself in school and a field-by-field employment
outlook for the woman college graduate through 1980.

EVERYWOMAN'S GUIDE TO POLITICAL AWARENESS
Phyllis Butler and Dorothy Gray
128 pages $3.95

This is a fact-filled handbook for all women who want a positive
introduction to institutional and power politics. It reviews the political structure, types of activity (volunteer, political, pro, candidate),
how to get involved, basic do's and dont's, the running of a cam-
paign, and much much more.

EVERYWOMAN'S GUIDE TO FINANCIAL INDEPENDENCE
Mavis Arthur Groza
144 pages $3.95

Rich or poor, single or married, every woman's questions about how
to handle finances are answered in this comprehensive money book.
It covers investing, budgeting, credit, insurance, estate planning,
saving and security, as well as the new credit laws and government
programs affecting the monetary concerns of women.

EVERYWOMAN'S GUIDE TO A NEW IMAGE
Peggy Granger
128 pages $3.95

This practical guide presents a range of new ideas - from bioenergetic
analysis to I Ching to humanistic psychology - along with a series of
interviews with women who have sucessfully translated these theories
into practical and meaningful changes in their lives.